WHEN THERE ARE NO WORDS

WHEN THERE ARE NO WORDS

SOUND THERAPY AND MUSIC AS MEDICINE

CAROL COLACURCIO

Copyright © 2019 by Carol Colacurcio.

ISBN:	Softcover	978-1-7960-6660-9
	eBook	978-1-7960-6659-3

All rights reserved. No part of this book may be reproduced or transmitted in any form or by any means, electronic or mechanical, including photocopying, recording, or by any information storage and retrieval system, without permission in writing from the copyright owner.

Any people depicted in stock imagery provided by Getty Images are models, and such images are being used for illustrative purposes only.
Certain stock imagery © Getty Images.

Scripture quotations marked NASB are taken from the New American Standard Bible®, Copyright © 1960, 1962, 1963, 1968, 1971, 1972, 1973, 1975, 1977, 1995 by The Lockman Foundation. Used by permission.

Cover photo by Dave Nutini
Carol's photo by Lauren Crank Colacurcio

Print information available on the last page.

Rev. date: 10/25/2019

To order additional copies of this book, contact:
Xlibris
1-888-795-4274
www.Xlibris.com
Orders@Xlibris.com
794013

TABLE OF CONTENTS

Dedication vii
Preface xi
Introduction xiii
Acknowledgements xvii

Chapter 1   How I Became Interested 1
Chapter 2   How Sound Works as Medicine 3
Chapter 3   Healing with Music 6
Chapter 4   Sound—A Vital Element for Health 10
Chapter 5   When There Are No Words 13
Chapter 6   How Music Works with Body, Mind and Spirit 18
Chapter 7   Listening 23
Chapter 8   Stories of Clients 29
Chapter 9   Using Music to Support the Grieving Process 56
Chapter 10   Grief and Using Specific Music for
              Release: The Bija Mantras 60
Chapter 11   Celia 63
Chapter 12   Hospice—Death and Dying 69
Chapter 13   Tibetan Singing Bowls 72
Chapter 14   Why Choose Certain Music and Instruments? 77
Chapter 15   The Chakras 84
Chapter 16   The First Chakra (Base of the Spine, Earth,) 87
Chapter 17   The Second Chakra (Below the navel, Water) 90
Chapter 18   The Third Chakra (Solar Plexis, Fire) 93
Chapter 19   The Fourth Chakra (Heart, Unconditional Love, Air) 97
Chapter 20   The Fifth Chakra (Throat, Sound) 104

Chapter 21 The Sixth Chakra (Third Eye, the
             Brow, Light, Inner Sound) 107
Chapter 22 The Seventh Chakra (Crown of head,
             Source to Connection, Divine Wisdom) 110
Chapter 23 Summary of the Chakras 114

Bija Mantras, Chakras and Toning... 116
Chakra Chart 117
Resource List of Music.. 120

Afterword 123
Final Dedication 125

Dedication

For Celia, my dearest professional colleague and friend, who helped me write this book "in absentia."

Dedication Prayer

By this effort may all sentient beings be free of suffering.
May their minds be filled with the nectar of virtue.
In this way may all causes resulting in suffering be extinguished,
And only the light of compassion shine throughout all realms

Preface

After practicing with sacred sound and music since the mid 90s, I have learned that the key for this work is in the listening. Not only is that my main concern as a practitioner, but also the client has the responsibility to listen. Having this kind of focus in listening guides one to know that the answers are within.

We have been conditioned to listen so as to give the "right" answers. True listening is silencing the chatter in the mind, letting the thoughts go that don't need attention at the moment, and being open and receptive to what does need attention. One learns to trust that the answers are there. More questions will surface, and so will the answers. The key is learning how to listen and trust.

We rely on outside sources to get information about what we need to relieve our pain, our emotional distress or mental confusion. Sometimes that is helpful but an even fuller awareness of our inner healer can provide the exact clues and information to get the answers that are key for ourselves.

That kind of information will be a little different for everyone because we all have pieces like puzzles to our lives that only we can put together. In the sound practice, I have found that a person's own images or internal information comes forth in journeying with sacred music. This kind of information is the exact key to unlock, face and let go/release any strong reactions. Then there is space to really be more present. There arises a deeper awareness that connects one with the divine within. There is a true knowing and trusting of our non-dual nature.

These themes and the methods that produce these results are what this book is about. The book itself is a journey.

Introduction

Music back in the 1960's was mostly thought of as entertainment. I was trained in the classical mode but did have interest in the music being played on the radio. Music was making major changes at this time, with Elvis Presley incorporating rock and roll sounds and movements. The Beatles made their appearance in the United States on the Ed Sullivan show in the mid sixties. Besides the 33rpm records, we could now buy 45rpm single records. All of this was a major influence on music, and of course how it has continued to develop since then.

I knew music was a way for me to express myself when there are no words. But I had no idea back then that there actually were music pieces and sounds that just by hearing and feeling the vibration caused mental release and spaciousness. As I became interested in using music as a way to calm the mind and heart, I discovered sound practitioners all over the world who had been doing this. There were sound healers in the third world villages who were the physicians. Their sounds or songs were passed down going back many generations. Some sound healers received their songs along their spiritual path and when sung definitely had healing effects. I wanted to learn more about using music this way. What sounds had which effects? What effect did different instruments have on the mind and body? Why did their songs work when the popular songs I love would not? How did one learn the skill to choose certain songs for particular healing purposes?

This book is about my journey through sound and music, and what I discovered on this path. My path with music became intertwined with my spiritual path. The guidance offered here is from my teachers from both of these paths. Music is where I had always felt "at home" and I learned to deepen in my spiritual path. There are specific practices in each, and doing the practices with discipline and an open heart led me to a fuller life of compassion.

In writing this book about my journey, I know of many others who connect strongly to music as medicine. The music sessions are powerful. I witness people having a quieter mind when listening to sacred music. They connect to the inner heart and find their way home. All beings experience busyness of the mind. The conceptual dimension of mind has the tendency to take over and fill one with constant thoughts and distractions. This makes one feel like there is a lot going on, but it is the busy mind that is in control, not you. By using sacred music, one notices that busyness and can begin to not engage with it. In doing so, the mind slowly settles. This leads to a calmer, happier and more spacious outlook that gives the self a sense of connection to the larger picture. Jane Roberts in The Nature of Personal Reality writes "Your joy, vitality and accomplishment do not come from the outside to you as the result of events that 'happen to you.' These qualities spring from inner events that are the result of your beliefs." Using your conscious mind to examine your beliefs, such as ones learned from parents, that do originate from outside you is necessary. But true joy and vitality do not come to you as a result of what comes from outside. There is the need for one to direct the conceptual mind to connect with what comes to you from within. Key to this is examining one's beliefs which are accessible in the contents of your own mind. One's imagination comes out of those beliefs as well as one's emotions. These beliefs can be broken through, even though they have become strong habits learned from childhood. These unexamined beliefs are accessible contents to your conceptual mind. When these beliefs go unexamined, there cannot be true spontaneity. In examining those beliefs from within, the information can open up a spaciousness and deeper connection to the truth of one's being. This is where the true experience of oneself is.

Sacred music accesses this place. It does its profound work as it by-passes the limitations of the conceptual mind. This is where the heart of the matter is. This is where change really takes place, and where one discovers the divine as your deepest source and resource.

I invite you to take your own inner journey. This book can open those inner doors using the vocal exercises, discovering how to listen and giving your most generous attention to sacred sounds. The music of sacred sounds is meant to open more fully the things one holds locked deep within. The journey guided by sacred sound can bring one into a calmer, more peaceful state of being where change does truly happen.

As Sogyal Rinpoche so lovingly reminds us with his teaching, "To Remember to remember to remember…"

Acknowledgements

Gratitude has to first go to my parents who were very supportive of my career in music. My mother inspired me when I was very young. Her own piano playing of Gershwin and Rachmaninoff was so beautiful and comforting to hear in the evenings. Mom started me on piano lessons with Betty Lukashuk when I was in first grade, studying with her for twelve years. Betty and her husband, Vladimir "Lucky", were my music parents. Lucky played violin with the Cincinnati Symphony and I was able to hear many excellent musicians. Lucky always invited me backstage to meet some of the musicians. It was amazing and exciting and I wanted to be a part of this kind of life. Thank you.

I also wish to acknowledge and thank the music school and all the teachers I had at Indiana University. The education there was intense, comprehensive and invaluable.

I want to thank all the students I have taught over the years and their wonderful parents. I felt a "family bond" with all of you.

Thank you to Pat Cook for the training in "Cross Cultural Sacred Music for Therapeutic Application." After that training and doing sessions with sacred music, I slowly began improvising piano for sessions. The advice from one of my teachers, Jetsunma Akon Lhamo, was invaluable on how to do this. She encouraged me to compose from a place of emptiness, really get myself out of the way. I wish to thank my Vajrayana teachers for the teachings and practices on meditation and mindfulness.

The move toward spontaneous playing led to recording some of these pieces. To Yeshe Phil Carbo who recorded my first pieces, a big thanks. Bill Danner produced and recorded my first CD called "Sound Accord." Other CDs that came next were "Tibetan Singing Bowls," "Music for the Archetypes," "Dreams of the Sun" and "Melodies of the Night." These were all produced and recorded by Mannie Garcia. Mike Powell helped with putting together the final production of my most recent CD "Melodies of the Night." I am most sincerely grateful to you all.

Most importantly, my gratitude overflows for my family. I have two amazing sons and daughters in law who produced eight lovely grandchildren. Before my first grandson was born, my daughter in law, Lauren, suggested I write music for the coming grandchildren. I wondered how many there would be! There are eight (5 boys and 3 girls), and I did compose for each their own lullaby. You can listen to them on the CD "Melodies of the Night."

And to my husband, Bob, I am so grateful for his loving support in this project. He has expertise in this area, being the writer in the family and having written seventeen books which are all published. He helped me with editing, organizing the material and clarifying the information. His help made this book move along smoothly. For me, I enjoyed the experience, seeing the process which made it fun doing the work together.

"When there are no words"

How I Became Interested

When I think back on my life, music has always been at the core of it. The times I was away from music, when my job was at a desk for example, never lasted that long. I always came back to playing or teaching music.

In the evening when my parents put us to bed, I'd be lying there with the thoughts and experiences of the day. The sweet sounds of my mom's piano would float up to my room, usually a piece by Gershwin such as Rhapsody in Blue or one of his preludes. My mother grew up taking piano lessons and learned to play quite well. Every evening she would play the piano probably for her sanity after a day with four children, but I truly relaxed when hearing these new sounds. The effect it had on me was feeling totally safe and enveloped by these beautiful sounds. There was an immediate calming effect, and pretty soon I was asleep even before the music stopped.

I think my mother wanted someone to continue with music so she had my brother start taking lessons. He would come home and practice piano, and I would listen and watch what he was doing. By the time I began lessons, I was already reading music. My training was in classical music, and I learned songs by many composers. I remember one year where I didn't want to practice. But after that, I enjoyed the challenge of learning each piece. After twelve years with my teacher, Betty Lukashuk, my only choice for college was music as it was my deepest love.

I was accepted to the music school, at Indiana University in Bloomington, Indiana. Step one was to audition. I also had to audition for a private teacher. Betty Lukashuk knew of the teacher, Jorge Bolet and told me to go see him. He told me that his schedule was full but did recommend another teacher, Tong Il Han. I studied with Mr. Han (from Korea) for two years. Another teacher, Alberto Reyes (from Uruguay) taught me after that. In looking back at this, my experience with music and people was becoming more cross cultural. Indiana was a perfect place to immerse myself into music. When one is in the music school, the only courses you take are music courses such as theory, chorus, music history, etc. There are concerts going on all the time. Students perform their recitals which are part of the program. There are orchestral concerts and operas. The teachers also give concerts as part of their performance schedules. I took advantage of all of these offerings.

After graduation, my plan was to teach piano privately. I moved back to northern Kentucky and began doing just that. There was also an opening at my high school to teach the music classes from grade one through sophomore levels. That was a very interesting experience as I learned that each grade level had its own way of learning, and so I learned a lot about how to approach each grade's listening abilities and challenges. This skill has proved invaluable.

How Sound Works as Medicine

Music is a natural mix of harmony, interconnection, life and breath. It engages both our emotional and intellectual sides; this in turn elevates the spirit. The sound healers were the physicians and did their healing by specific songs and sounds as the prescribed medicine. These healers were giving vital energy to the body causing a dynamic change to take place. This kind of music as medicine can actually make changes at the cellular level. The cells can become more fully awakened and working to support the body, mind and spirit.

Another way sound works is by entrainment. This method is used to slow down the heart rate, breath and the mental activity. When I led a bereavement group that had widows and widowers whose spouses had died recently, there were always comments about not being able to fall asleep or waking up at three am, also known as the "grieving hour." I recommended a CD by Janalea Hoffman called <u>Musical Acupuncture</u>. Janalea composed this music in which the rhythms are at eighty beats a minute; this matches a human's normal heart rate during the day. She very gently slows the beat down to fifty. The people in my group who used this CD had great success and recommended it to any newcomers. We humans wish to be "in sync" with ourselves and others. This is called entrainment. Here are a couple of other examples of entrainment: a surgeon was performing a transplant and the donor and patient were side by side in the surgery room. As the procedure began, the surgeon noticed that the heart rates of the patient and donor began to beat in exact sync. Another example is about a clockmaker who had many clocks in a large room. He wound them in the evening and they were all ticking at their own time. In the morning when he went back to the room, all of the clocks were beating together.

Entrainment brings one into a more balanced breathing pattern. In fact, any and all bodily rhythms can be positively affected by entrainment. Having our bodies, breath and mental state be calmer and more balanced creates space to release old energies, and we feel the results of becoming more relaxed and peaceful.

Listening is an active skill which we are not typically taught. When someone says to listen, most of us shut down a bit and keep silent, and inadvertently react to what is being said in some way. Another bad habit is to interrupt because we want to get our thoughts spoken out loud. Rather than allowing our thoughts to wander and thinking about what we want to say next, there should be active attention and focus on what the speaker is saying. One of the most generous gifts is to offer another our complete undivided attention. So, allow your mind to be quiet. Listening consciously can expand our minds and improve one's health. According to Julian Treasure, a sound and communication expert who gives talks on effective listening, there are four ways sound affects us:

1. physiological—sounds can adversely affect our heart rate, brain waves and breathing. For example, a loud crash or alarm can jar us where nature sounds as lapping waves and wind in the trees can soothe us.
2. psychological—hearing music gives rise to different emotional states. For example, bird calls feel reassuring and safe. Finger nails on a chalk board are almost universally experienced as grating on the nerves.
3. cognitive—multitasking to the contrary not withstanding, our minds can really only do one thing at a time. Nevertheless, we are surrounded often by talking, traffic, audio, video and other ambient sounds. Productivity is often adversely affected by this.

4. behavioral—we tend to move physically or emotionally toward pleasant sounds. Long exposure to harsh sounds has the opposite effect and can be damaging to one's health.

Listening is the doorway to understanding. There are two ways we listen:

1. Reductive listening (listening for something…). Men characteristically listen this way. They are listening for "Here's the problem, break down the information to find the solution, Ok, what's next?"
2. Expansive listening (listening with…). Women typically listen this way. They usually face each other and enjoy the journey as they talk. Ok, sometimes they talk at the same time.

Sometimes listening is made difficult either by exterior or interior noise. Big cities have noise going on day and night. People living in or visiting noisy cities frequently report having more sleep problems than people living in quiet rural areas. Technology is the culprit, as the number of cars has increased creating more traffic, and there are also more airplanes, snowmobiles, motorcycles and trucks. In the cities, there is also construction, night time noises, horns, buses and trains. Some cities have noise legislation trying to reduce noise pollution on Sunday. The ringing of church bells in some cities has been restricted to certain times. For a wonderful history on this topic, see <u>The Soundscape: Our Sonic Environment and the Tuning of the World</u> by R. Murray Schafer, 1977, 1994. Wind, water, birds and silence are all "friends" of sound. Think about creating a soundscape of your own. Around the outside of my home, are strategically placed tuned wind chimes, as an example. In our neighborhood, people have commented on the relaxing feeling when they hear wind chimes which blend high and low tones. In most urban environments, therefore, it requires effort to practice conscious listening, but since it opens the doorway to deeper understanding, I feel it is worth the effort.

Healing with Music

Our favorite music can calm us or energize us to help us get through our day. But have you thought about using music to relieve pain or help to manage stress? How about using music and sound for expressing difficult emotions (as grieving) or to improve concentration and creativity?

Sound and music as "medicine" is universal. It is part of every great spiritual system, and has been used as a healing method by the indigenous cultures for thousands of years. In the indigenous tradition, the sound healers in their villages were the physicians. Their knowledge of sound was passed down from generation to generation. Sometimes a healer had a song that came through an experience like divine inspiration. Their intention is always to benefit and heal. For example, Kanacus Littlefish, a Native American medicine man, has a song for dealing with serious illness. One of my clients was dealing with cancer. When I first played this piece for him, war imagery arose in his mind. He didn't like the piece because it brought up all his anger from the war. I continued to play this piece for him over a period of three months. At that point, his response to this piece was a feeling of relaxation and a calmness.

The benefits of healing sounds through active listening, toning and Tibetan singing bowls can be experienced immediately. This is listening to music, not as entertainment, but with a different approach and attitude. It doesn't matter if you like or don't like the sounds. This is about listening and observing where the sound goes and what comes up such as imagery, memories, emotions, etc. This is <u>listening without the internal critic, there are no judgments.</u> This music helps one to by-pass all the mental noise, worries and fears that get in the way. This type of listening allows "answers" to arise from a deeper place and space.

Why use sacred sounds? The intention as well as the natural dynamism of this kind of music is to promote change: 1. For health and healing 2. For resolving difficult emotions 3. For the time of death and transition.

The vibration of these kinds of sounds (Bija mantras, toning for example) fosters change and causes healing movement in the body/mind complex. Using music in this way is a <u>support</u> for the person especially when dealing with difficult, strenuous and heavy issues. Sacred music can help one find a way to the healing of greater clarity and peace. The healing environment created by sacred sound is totally free from the feeling of judgment, misunderstanding and misinterpretation that often occurs within interpersonal therapies.

When I do a session, I find out what the issue is and the emotions around that. I have the client do some vocal toning to hear how they sound. As they make sounds, I ask them to listen and experience the deep resonance of these sounds: 1. Feel and observe the effect this has on oneself 2. Listen without judgment or criticism 3. Observe whatever is noticeable. The intention of the sacred sound is to go where it is needed. It by-passes the judgmental mind so we don't get caught in our thoughts and conceptual elaborations. What comes up is the perfect information for the person at that time.

Sound and sacred music work because things are constantly changing within and around us. The music I use as a sound healer creates intentional movement towards harmonic change. Clear awareness is brought into play so that constricting thoughts and emotions respond naturally towards release and relaxation.

I have found that sacred sound and music is applicable for many situations: writers block, blood pressure, stress relief, sleep problems, pain, grief, old fears/patterns, abuse, traumas, A.D.D., meditation and hospice. In hospice, I had the privilege of bringing relief to patients suffering from cancer, Alzheimers and ALS. And of course, sacred sound creates an especially peaceful environment that eases the transition of the dying person.

What Sacred Sounds Do

1. They improve synapse response in the brain.
2. They stimulate the immune system.
3. They are used to calm the mind and bring stability to the body.
4. They are used for meditation, ADHD and oncology.
5. They help induce semi-trance to do inner journeying.
6. They have power and energy to stimulate the entire psychosomatic system.
(reference from Sacred Sounds, Transformation through Music & Word by Ted Andrews, 1992).

Discover Your Inner Journey

We pay a lot of attention to the outside world and respond to it constantly. Our many life experiences accumulate and create a source from which we respond and react. With sacred sounds and music, we can go a bit deeper and get beyond reactions to habitual everyday experience.

The healing of our frustrations, the curbing of our anger and fears comes from this deeper place within us. This "place" is the divine essence or the luminous energy body. Sacred sound/music can help us connect with that place. In a few music journeys, the experience can go from being in a dark closet, hungry and dirty to a beautiful, sunny mountain with white clouds in the blue sky. In that place one can experience a special spaciousness from which to experience the divine in a new way. In this special place we become momentarily free from our usual everyday limitations.

Time in this place is especially open and free from the usual clock-time constraints. Rest comes easy there. The usual pressure to engage the mind in thinking, judging, criticizing or analyzing is relaxed and released. Resting in this place, it is easy simply to observe what bubbles up from our sacred depths. Listening in this way is a new experience for most. Through this kind of listening, one can experience something naturally deeper but more sacred. The divine luminous energy body, which is beyond one's usual self imposed limitations, makes itself known easily and naturally when one rests in a place of perfect peace.

Sound—A Vital Element for Health

Balance, as opposed to overdoing it, is important in anything we do and especially in one's sound health. Sound affects every part of our body and mind. Music is in every part of one's brain. If a person looses part of their brain function, there still is the capacity to hear music. One of the diagnostic tools I use is a sound scan. This is so I can hear what sounds are "missing." The person begins by making a low tone and slides up to the highest tone, then slides back down to the low tone. Over the 20 years I've been doing this work, very few people can produce the full range. I have heard the low range totally missing, and the high range not able to be vocalized in some, and then the middle range being skipped over too.

Music affects us through rhythm, harmony and melody/movement. When you feel: 1. Melody or movement with music, you are following the sound that brings one from beginning to end. With the final chord or the conclusion of sound, there is release of stress, strong emotions and pain. Examples of music I have used are <u>Points of Light</u> by Boris Mourashkin, 1995 or <u>Rivers of One</u>, Traditional Sufi Healing Music, Interworld Music Associates. Other suggestions in general are Gregorian chant, India classical tradition, Native American flute, alto flute, piano, and strings such as cello, violin and harp. 2. Rhythm is the beat, a strong regular repeated flow in music that creates a pattern of sound. If one is feeling "off," scattered mentally or ones breathing is shallow, rhythm can bring one back to balance and safety.

Drums are an effective instrument to entrain to a regular rhythm. One of my favorite CDs using drums effectively for healing is <u>Rhythm of the Chakras</u> by Glen Valez, Sounds True 1998. 3. Harmony is the third element of music that creates movement and dissonance to resolution. Harmony is the use and study of chords and their progressions. Chords are the playing of two or more notes at one time. There are many choices but I would like to mention a few; <u>Chinese Feng Shui Music,</u> 1995 from Wind Records; <u>Music from Health Journeys 1992 &1997</u> and <u>Inward Journey</u>, 2003, from Image Paths. These are longer musical healing pieces for inner journeying. Other instruments in general for music with harmony are piano, ragas, harp and Tibetan singing bowls.

To understand "music as medicine" I direct a person to listen and observe without judgment. Notice what comes up mentally, physically or emotionally. Let it happen, face it and let it be. I write down what is coming up for the person so we can discuss it after the session. Some thoughts and questions to pose are: What makes you angry, prideful or lonely? One can use the meditation technique to face those fears, befriend it or just allow it to be. Recognize these habits as old reactions that still play out. They can be put to rest. One develops courage when facing adversity.

I have found that what comes up for each person is what they were talking about when they came in the door. The information they get is exactly what they are working on. There are sound practices they can work on at home to help maintain a healthier sound body and mind. I would recommend the Bija Mantras (see resources in the back), sacred primordial sounds of Om, Ah and Hung, and the tones used with each chakra. These are chanted and directed to the area of the body:

<u>Toning the Chakras</u>

1. Long U vowel or OM (circulatory system)
2. Long O or OM (muscle system)

3. Awh or AH (digestive system)
4. Long A or AH (immune system)
5. Long Ay (respiratory, glands)
6. Long Ee (pituitary gland, endocrine system,
7. Eyes, ears, nose throat)
8. Long Ee (nervous system, skeletal system)

Tonglen is a breath meditation practice. It is often referred to as "giving and receiving," where one takes in the suffering of the world with an inhalation, and breathes out comfort, healing and compassion. When we take in others' pain with an in-breath and send benefit on the out-breath, this antidotes one's own selfishness. This practice helps liberate one from old selfish patterns so there can be a more loving feeling toward self and others. When we see others suffering, we are reminded of our own confusion, fear and anger. In doing Tonglen, when one breathes in for all and breathes out for all, that is the beginning to understand suffering in the world more deeply. Breathe in their pain and send them relief. Subtle changes will begin to take place in one's thinking patterns. Gradually, you will find your capacity for kindness increasing where before, loving kindness towards all seemed like an impossible stretch.

When There Are No Words

Sound therapy is about the use of tones or sounds to improve health. Certain tones, music and sounds can help to release the emotional hold on our minds. A person hears the sounds and responds to them. This is not about liking the music. The critical part of the brain is not where listening is localized. Sound therapy directs one's attention to listening fully (not just with the brain) and to noticing where the sounds go and how one responds.

Listening is an active skill which we are not taught. There is so much noise that goes on around us that can cause problems with sleep, pain and stress. Friendly sounds are wind, water, birds and silence.

My training comes from the indigenous sacred sound tradition that uses particular sounds or instruments for healing. When one listens to this kind of sound/music it brings up unexpected responses. Some people get an energy response, others a story from their past ("I don't know why this came up but...."), some an image of a place one has never been before. These responses do not come from the conceptual or discursive part of the brain. What comes up turns out to be a piece of the puzzle that helps one understand why their current problem persists. The music/sounds bring up things that help one resolve an issue. I realized this works so well because the answers the person needs come from inside them, not from any outside source, including me. No one is telling them to try or do something. They get the answer that is perfect for the issue they came to work on using sacred sound as their guide.

I have asked a few of the people I've done extensive music sessions with if I could share some of their experiences. They have given me permission. I feel it is so important to share what these people learned from their sound sessions and the imagery that led them to their own revelations. Many of these people I met while working as a hospice caretaker. Let me start with A. I went to visit him at his home. At this point he was confined to a special chair because he had ALS. We had a lot in common, both of us being musicians. He had a piano so I was able to play live music for him. He was a woodworker, photographer and avid reader. We never lacked for conversation. We both liked to discuss spiritual paths and perspectives on how to follow those paths.

I had all kinds of music for him to experience as well as my original music to play to get his responses. I played Tibetan singing bowls that gave him release. He said he felt more spacious. I would put the bowls on his legs and around his chair and just play them. He would close his eyes and just let the sound fully surround and go through him.

L. I met her only three times. She was the mother of one of my friends. The first time I met her, I was visiting my friend when L. stopped by. I noticed how she stood tall and moved so gracefully. She reminded me of Katherine Hepburn. She mingled easily with her daughters. She was a picture of strength and beauty. The second time I met L was in the hospice home. She was still able to sit in a chair but the Alzheimer's had taken its toll on her memory. My friend asked if I would do some music with her mother. I played a piece as background sound that was relaxing for her. I also had four Tibetan singing bowls. I put a couple in her lap and held a bowl near her. L mostly had her eyes closed and when I started to play the bowl, her face wore a frown. When the bowls sung their special harmonics, her brow unknit and her face relaxed. The third time with L was the evening of her death. My friend asked a group of us to do prayers and chants. I played my singing bowls. This time, I held the large bowl at her heart. I placed a smaller bowl at the crown of her head. These were gently rung and continued to vibrate. We began the prayers, then ended with ringing the bowls. She died peacefully three hours later. J. My husband, also a hospice caretaker, had been visiting J. He was interested in the music work so I went to do some sessions with him. He was dealing with AIDS so we worked on dealing with his pain, indigestion and circulation. He knew his time to die was coming soon, so we prepared him for the time of his parting. He told me the piece he wished played at the time of his death. Sometime later, we got the call that he was unconscious and was taken to the hospital. We drove to the hospital. I had been keeping a boombox in the car and the sacred music he wanted played as he was dying. In the room, we were playing the music and we were praying. He died peacefully with all of this around him. His wish was accomplished.

 J. I was asked to sit with her and was told she was near death. She was not conscious, and was scrunched up on her side. There was no verbal communication. I brought a couple singing bowls. I played one in my hand and the other I placed at the crown of her head. When I played it gently, her brow unfurled and she rolled on her back straightening her body. She seemed to be more relaxed. I continued to pray and play the bowls. She died two hours later.

 O. I met O in a nursing home. She was totally bedbound, always sitting up to talk and sleeping that way, supported by the bed and pillows. She had been that way for two years. She was a vibrant woman and an artist. She continued to do her art even in this condition. She insisted that I bring the singing bowls whenever I visited. She loved the harmonies, the relaxed feelings and easing of tensions the bowls gave her. She would lose herself in the sounds. Oftentimes my visits simply consisted of playing the bowls. If anyone went by her door, she would tell me, "They need these. They are so tense." She would invite them in to experience the sounds. As she became progressively weaker and was not talking at all, I would still play the bowls. She would slowly raise her head and smile. The last time I was with her, I put a bowl on each of her shoulders to ease her. She became totally absorbed in the sound and vibration. Then she said, "Tomorrow," and

I said "I'll come back tomorrow." She smiled and her head relaxed down again. When I left, I gave her a hug and told her "I love you" and she said "I love you." That was all. I was ready to go back early the next morning, but got a phone call from hospice telling me O had died.

CT. I got word that CT wanted to see me as she had heard about this sound work I was doing. I loved being with her, hearing about her life and learning about what she was dealing with. I did many music sessions with her and she would tell me they were wonderful and very helpful. She offered me an "official" testimonial, which I recorded. Here is what she said: "I have a rare disease called amyloidosis and it gives me extreme pains a lot of the time and I wear a pump filled with morphine so as to control that pain. Lately it hasn't been doing that. So, Carol has been helping me by doing music therapy. And I'm amazed every time, Carol, at what you do because it follows a pattern every time which is very similar.

"First of all, I don't really expect it to work and just think it is a nice relaxation technique. I can't understand how just vibrations would do what you hope they would do which is appease pain and make you feel better and so on.

"So I just lie down and relax and listen and the first moments, despite myself, are very emotional always. Just wanting to cry or sometimes crying and also always an exacerbation of the pain for a good three-four minutes. And then little by little, I sort of even out, and the pain evens out with me. I relax and thoughts come to my mind or pictures or words that really come to the forefront of my mind. I've talked to you about them afterwards; they always have a deep meaning of which I was not aware at all.

"And when the session is over, I just feel so energized, so well and the pain hasn't disappeared because it is extremely severe but it is so much better, and it is manageable and it has taken a back seat in my life. And so it's just wonderful. And that happens every time we've had a session, it isn't just a fluke or accident that has happened once. We've had several sessions now. Every time I've had that and always in the same pattern, always going in the same format.

"So I'm very, very thankful. And these effects last quite a while, they last several days after the session. And I reinforce them by listening to the tapes you've made me at home. So all in all, keeping on top of it, thanks to you. Thank you, Carol."

In conclusion, I hope it is obvious that the relaxation and release from stress and pain that these hospice patients experienced was not from anything I said. With the dying patient especially, there often are no words. Nevertheless, there was a rich and full communication taking place because of the sacred sound. And that communication was not primarily with me. It was a silent internal "dialog" on the part of the patient that revealed many precious and peaceful things that greatly eased their dying process and passing over.

How Music Works with Body, Mind and Spirit

As I mentioned, after college I began to teach private piano lessons as well as teach music in a high school. Because of my husband's work, we moved a few times. I was always able to find new piano students. Since I had time during the day (most of my lessons were after 3pm) so I began to volunteer at a hospice. It occurred to me that music had been therapeutic for me through my life, and I wondered how I could learn more about how to use music as a healing tool. Pursuing that line of thought, I found a training in Seattle, Washington about using cross cultural music as therapy. Over a year's time, I studied and experienced all kinds of sacred music from different cultures worldwide. There was a lot of listening to hear and feel the effects on the body and mind. Different kinds of instruments would have certain effects on different parts of the body. We learned how the indigenous healers sung or played longer pieces to help with particular problems such as abuse, anger, grief and other deep emotional residues left over from traumas of one kind or another. After I completed my certification in using cross cultural music for therapeutic applications, I had the new tools but wondered where my new skills might lead. Also I wondered what else I might need to know. I read many books on sound to explain how and why it works as "medicine." Let me now list some of these:

1. Robert Jourdain, Music, The Brain, and Ecstasy: How Music Captures Our Imagination (William Morrow and Company, Inc., New York, 1997)
2. Joachim-Ernst Berendt, The Third Ear: On Listening To The World (Henry Holt and Company, Inc., 1985)
3. Joachim-Ernst Berendt, The World is Sound: Nada Brahma: Music and the Landscape of Consciousness (Destiny Books, Rochester, Vermont, 1983).
4. Julia Schnebly-Black, Ph.D. and Stephen F. Moore, PhD., The Rhythm Inside: Connecting Body, Mind, and Spirit Through Music (Rudra Press, Portland, Oregon, 1997)
5. R. Murray Schafer, The Soundscape: Our Sonic Environment and the Tuning of the World (Destiny Books, Rochester, Vermont, 1977)
6. Joshua Leeds, The Power of Sound: How to Manage Your Personal Soundscape for a Vital, Productive, & Healthy Life (Healing Arts Press, Rochester, Vermont, 2001)

This information about sound and why it works helped me understand the effects music had on me all these years.

I learned that the sound healers received their songs by spiritual revelation. These sacred melodies passed down from generation to generation. I wondered how these sounds might work on westerners having a very different cultural background. In the West, we have learned to use music for entertainment. It can stimulate or help one relax, and of course, everyone has their favorite music to play as their ultimate fallback in times of stress. But what happens when your favorite music doesn't have the hoped for effect? Helen Bonny, founder of GIM, (Guided Imagery and Music) discovered this for herself. She became ill and was in the hospital. She asked her son to bring her favorite classical pieces. She was curious as to why they weren't comforting and she didn't wish to hear them. They were not pleasing and comforting as she had hoped. This brought her to study more about how music works on a different level of healing.

The sacred sounds of the healers from around the world are now coming to the West. I have given talks to many groups in such diverse fields as medical, social service, hospice and meditation practitioners; and there needs to be education for therapists, doctors, nurses, counselors, social workers and others about how to use sound as a medical therapy. The professionals I've teamed up with have seen the profound effects and results from this kind of music. There will be chapters later about working with hospice, grieving and bereavement, which is where I draw the bulk of my experience. There will also be chapters on the archetypes, the chakras, toning, singing bowls and imagery.

Music is audible vibration. Our bodies are set up in the same ratios that relate to intervals in music. An interval is the distance between two tones. When we hear an interval, our body and nervous system resonate and entrain to it. For example, you can see on a piano that the distance between middle C and the C above is an octave or eight notes apart. This is a ratio of 2:1. From our head to our toes is also a ratio of 2:1. "In essence, you can tune your body like a musical instrument. These tones resonate with the flow and energies of our bodies and so the body can realign itself." (Calendula CD by John Beaulieu).

Another way to see what is happening when we are aligning the body was demonstrated by a Swiss physician, artist and natural scientist, Dr. Hans Jenny (1904-1972). In the film, "Cybernetics," he showed how inert substances (sand, copper filings for example) formed patterns when sound vibrations were played from beneath. The results are beautiful images out of sand, liquids or powders that are stimulated by sound. They resemble snowflake designs, with a uniqueness and harmonious quality. If the effect of sacred sound makes these beautiful images out of sand, etc., imagine the vibration of these tones on yourself, and what kind of realignment is taking place in your circulation, nervous system and even to the cellular level.

In India, sacred music has been part of everyday life. There are sacred pieces called ragas, some to be only sung in the morning, others only sung in the evening. It is said that ragas are very foundational and are passed down to each new generation. From the spiritual traditions in India and Tibet, there are the sacred syllables OM, AH and HUNG. These are from Sanskrit which is a language with special qualities promoting spiritual healing and change. These are regarded as primordial sounds that bring harmony and balance to the entire psychosomatic system.

Toning is making sound/vibration (for example Om or Ah) until you need to take another breath, then take another breath and make the sound again. The pitch should be a comfortable place for your voice range. As you do this, let the sound resonate throughout your body. Notice where the sound goes. When you stop after a few minutes, notice the difference in how you feel. This easy practice can change and re-tune your system because that is the nature of sacred sound. Toning is using your own voice, and the vibration of the sacred syllables will balance the body. Using these elongated vowel sounds can improve the ability to listen.

Other benefits of toning are:

- receiving auditory information through the ear, skin and bones,
- a positive way for non-invasive physical and mental improvement,
- brain waves, muscle tension, heartbeat, blood pressure and pain are altered,
- vocal scanning (make the sound, then slide from low to high then back to low). This is a simple means of assessing the emotions, the body and the mind by hearing where the sound resonates strong or weak,
- practice of toning daily is effective in improving one's health.

The Bija mantras are another way to direct sound vibration to specific parts of the body. Doing chant repetition with each of these Sanskrit syllables helps to vibrate that area. It is like an inner body massage. Since these are sacred syllables, their vibration naturally promotes healing. There is a syllable corresponding to each of the chakras starting at the base and moving up to the crown:

1. Lam, 2. Vam, 3. Ram, 4. Yam, 5. Ham, 6. Aum, 7. Om. Chanting a few minutes daily can change ones vibration for the better.

There is an interesting movie called "As It Is In Heaven" about a young man in Sweden who leaves his small home town and becomes a world famous music conductor. He returns to his town later in life for health reasons. He spends most of his time alone. The main church in town asks him to be their conductor. He refuses at first but then eventually takes the job as cantor of the church which includes conducting the choir.

His choral techniques are very unusual and soon the choir is noticing their improvement. His way for them to dig deeper and find their "core" voice was to use movement, making sound, listening and releasing any places in the body where they felt blocked. One man was able to open up to a woman in the group, telling her that he had been in love with her since grade school. She never knew that and they did get together.

As these personal, deep feelings were revealed to the choir, a lot of judgment was let go. The ones who did not speak up realized that their silence was keeping others from opening up. The result was a very strong connection made among the members of the choir. Their voices reflected this inner change and the beauty of their new sound was astounding. The harmony was there with the clarity of their minds.

The deeper place offers unlimited information, clarity and wisdom to break through the blocks and confusion we have. Sacred sound is a way to reach that place. The flow from that is compassion and loving kindness toward all beings.

Listening

Hearing is constantly happening whether we want to hear or not. Unlike vision, where we can close our eyes, it is hard to stop hearing. Even if we cover our ears, we may still feel vibrations in our body.

Listening and hearing are very different. What do we hear when we are listening? Do you think you are really hearing the whole picture? Think about times you are listening to someone talk about a subject. How do you understand that information? Are you thinking of something to say as they are speaking? Have you missed some of the points they were making because your mind was somewhere else? How about the filter in our minds from our own points of view and experiences which cause us to jump to opinions, criticisms and other conclusions? So to what or whom are we really listening?

Our ears are the link between the world within and without. When listening doesn't develop, communication is cut off and problems arise such as speech impairments, hyperactivity, depression and autism. Have you ever had the experience of telling your story and you feel like you haven't been heard? Or someone takes it the wrong way? Emotions can compromise your listening capacity. Think about a time when you were angry or grieving. Those kinds of emotions tend to consume the mind entirely and one's energy completely, so you can see that listening takes a lot of concentration and focus. Improving one's listening can have profound ramifications on the way one thinks and interacts with the world. To really improve one's listening skills means working with the mind and silencing your thoughts when listening to someone. This is very similar to meditation practice. Someone who begins meditation thinks that you sit quietly and relax. When you actually do sit in the meditation posture, the mind suddenly takes over with a constant stream of thoughts. This may come as a surprise but actually it is happening all the time. We don't notice because we don't pay attention, and so we don't notice all that mental chatter. This is just a habit of mind and meditation is bringing awareness to break this habit and becoming familiar with it.

In meditation practice, one focuses on the breath and when thoughts arise, you let them rise and let them go. The thoughts are not the problem, rather it is our own engagement in the thoughts. When a thought arises, we think we have to do something with it. Then our mind begins to bubble, our emotions come into play, and we lose our focus entirely. This is just a habitual reaction. When this happens, the practice is to bring oneself back to your breath. After doing this for a time, one can catch the mind earlier from engaging with a thought. Eventually, one will stay with the breath and let the thoughts go. Once the mind has some experience with staying with the breath, then another aspect is to see what thought arises, examine it and the emotions around it, to find out what the underlying cause of that thought is. In other words, why did I have that reaction? Patterns will start to show. This is about learning about our own habits of mind that keep us stuck in certain thought forms. The good news is that a habit can be broken. We all know that takes a lot of fortitude and discipline. But once one begins to listen to the mind, to really hear what it is saying, then one examines why and where that came from. From there the practice is to let it rise and let it go. One does not need to engage in reacting to all that comes up in the mind. Just let it arise and no need to follow it. One then may experience some spaciousness and clarity, which will result in a different way of listening.

The sound work, as I explain and teach it, can aid in this process. Sound is energy, it nourishes our system. The music of the sacred sound tradition and music created for healing purposes is a gentle way to bring up certain memories, places and emotions that relate to a particular issue. For example, a single mom came to do a session and she told me that she felt very sad about her family life.

She didn't understand why, since she loved her daughter. Why was she feeling sadness? I chose a few pieces and had her relax with breathing; then she just let her mind go where it wanted. When the music stopped, I asked her if she had any comments. She related a vivid picture of her grandmother in a rocking chair. I asked her why did her grandmother show up, how did she feel about her? She told me that her grandmother broke up her family, was a negative and argumentative person. My client related this back to her own sadness, and saw that it had come from the strong negative emotions she absorbed from her grandmother. Once she could see that, she was able to let it go and function as the loving mom she wanted to be.

In doing music sessions, I have always found that the sounds by-pass the conceptual dimension of the mind. Sound can touch us deeply. Sound will go where it is needed, so it could release a memory or image or locate places of tension in the body. One does not know what will arise, so the "busy mind" simply gets by-passed. In other words, you are not deciding or judging what you will say or even what you will think. One allows the music to just happen. People report to me just what comes up. Having by-passed the judgmental frame of mind, the music allows a memory or thought that is connected to their issue to come up. **It is my experience that every time a person gets a memory, event, story, color or vision it is exactly what they need at that particular time for that particular issue.** The solution is perfect because it comes from the deepest healing resources of the persons themselves. I will be giving many examples in another chapter about results from sessions where this is in fact the case.

For now, here are some thoughts about healing with sound:

--We are a container, sound takes us to a larger place within and broadens our vision, so that we recognize we "contain" much more than we ever imagined,
--How much are we conscious of what we hear? (For example, when taking a walk do we really hear what is around us?)

--How much can we release, regulate and stabilize our energy so that it supports genuine listening rather than being an impediment?

--How do emotions compromise one's listening? What mental attitude underlies the particular emotional issue we struggle with?

Health is a condition where rhythm, harmony and tone are in perfect coordination. Music is rhythm, harmony and tone. Music can antidote an inner condition of illness even though outwardly we may feel fine. Eventually, the inner illness will surface in the body. This shows how important it is to change the thoughts and lift the heart out of the shadows. Music and sentient beings are both miniatures of the harmony that coordinates the energy and life of the universe.

"Music helps us to train ourselves in harmony, harmony with life. All good tendencies such as gentleness and tolerance, forgiveness, love and appreciation, all these beautiful qualities, come by being light; light in the mind, in the soul, and in the body.

Music helps sentient beings to concentrate or meditate independently of thought, and therefore music seems to be the bridge over the gulf between form and formless. It creates also that resonance which vibrates through the whole being, lifting the thought above the denseness of matter, a harmony of vibrations touching every atom of one's whole being. Music touches our innermost being and in that way produces new life, a life that gives exaltation to the whole being, the fulfillment of one's life." (from Music by Sufi Inayat Kyan).

How we listen is how we process.

One is happier and healthier when listening skills are improved. To begin to examine how you listen, here are some questions to think about after listening to a piece of music or the sounds of nature.

1. What instruments/sounds did you hear?
2. Did you feel any vibration or sensation physically?
3. Did the music sound more high or low? What did you notice?
4. Did the music sound too fast or slow? (rhythm)
5. Did the music evoke an emotion (happy, sad, fear, anger)?
6. Did any image or memory come to mind?
7. What posture were you in? (Laying down, sitting, meditative)
8. Was the music too overwhelming? (too many instruments). Or underwhelming? (solo instrument, simple harmony).
9. Did any colors appear?
10. Did you feel any movement around you or did you feel like moving?
11. Any other comments?

Examining the ways we listen can help us understand our own reactions. What reactions do we have? Do we like it or not, feel more relaxed or more tense, what emotions arise or what memories arise? Physically we might want to move around and feel more energy. Sound healing can "entrain" our rhythms back to their natural state. When you feel breathless or your heart is racing, sound can bring one back to the natural rhythm. And when one rhythm is regular, the others follow. We also may want to fall asleep or may feel more focused. When someone is speaking to you, really tune in to listen to their words, tone, loudness and softness. Notice if your thoughts get in the way before they finish speaking.

Another listening exercise is to close your eyes and open your sense of hearing to what is immediately around you. Then expand that sense beyond the room, the building, the yard, the community, the state, the country....you get the idea to keep opening and expanding the sense of hearing. Give yourself time to just dwell in the spacious place.

We are energy and we tune to it. Sound healing can help one find those places within, learn to trust this inner wisdom and reconnect on a deeper level.

Meditation with Music

From The Third Ear (pg 118) by David Bohm, atomic physicist: "What interferes with listening…is that thought jumps in very fast with a word and all its associations, which then goes so fast that thought takes that to be direct perception."

Our habit of mind is described in the above quote. We think we are engaging in a fresh way with others, but our mind actually is going by responses we have learned to accept or reject. Filtering through our minds to come to some conclusion is a "knee jerk" reaction. How do we sift through this, discard and let go, to bring a response from a deeper place? Meditation is a method for examining what we cling to mentally and emotionally, seeing it for what it is, and then practicing letting go. Spaciousness and clarity are the qualities that arise from a relaxed mind.

In the beginning when one meditates, one watches the mind to learn how it works. It may take some time to quiet the mind, and have it relax. Music and toning are a way to bring one to this kind of relaxed focus. The vibrations of different sounds have an effect like a massage on the inner body, calming and releasing accumulated stress. Vocal toning and listening for about ten to fifteen minutes a day can produce a more relaxed state. The mind will feel more spacious (open to listening) and less apt to judge so quickly. To listen from a more spacious place will open up one's creativity, insight and intuition. This is where the healing takes place.

Stories of Clients

JC—

We met "coincidently" at an office when she heard me talking to the nurse about sound and healing. When that conversation ended, I went out the front and JC was there waiting for me. She asked if I was a sound practitioner. I had been working on an easy name for my new profession and when she said "sound practitioner," I knew that was it! JC was one of my first clients and during our journey together, she became a dear friend.

We talked about why she wanted to work with sound/music. She was dealing with cancer, and had pelvic surgery done already. Her main concerns were about relaxation. Her work as a guidance counselor for K through fifth grade was very stressful. She had realized the stressful work she did was not helpful for slowing the growth of cancer. The beginning of our work together was focused on relaxation, toning, breathing with biofeedback music, releasing through therapeutic sounds ("Rhythm of Chakras" by Glen Velez) and evening out the session with a relaxing melody ("Song to Shiva" by Vyaas Houston and Mark Kelso).

JC was very spiritually minded and later, after much study, became a minister. In our music sessions, she began to have images of her spirit wanting to fly. There were still lots of tensions and stress she was working on. With some music (Karunamayee, India music) she felt the drum move up and down where she had pain. I played piano and she felt her breathing to be cooler, calmer and refreshed.

I asked her to capture some of the imagery of her journey, and make some drawings. She drew water with a dolphin and whale. There was a big tree next to the water. Birds were flying through the clouds in a blue sky. There was a hand coming up through the water, reaching up for something. She did not know what the hand was reaching for. I improvised on the piano for JC so that her journey might continue, and she again saw the moving water, the freedom of the dolphins and whales. She noticed the tree was firmly rooted. Then a hand reached down from the heavens to grasp hers in the water. That hand gave her great strength and was there to take her home.

JC's imagery continued throughout her sessions and she derived strength and found greater spaciousness. Sometimes she would be kayaking, which she loved to do, relaxing on the water, enjoying a red/yellow sunset. In one session, she started with tenseness, headache and a cold. I played Tibetan singing bowls for her which felt uncomfortable that day. Next I played a piece called 'Joy/Hope' by Boris Mourashkin. This brought her to walking along the beach, birds soaring through the air, whiteness, cool, peaceful.

Her journey continued in a marsh, searching for which way to go. She felt bursts of white feeling in the second chakra. It was both irritating and pleasant. She found she would tense up when she didn't like the sound, but then let it go—letting it be just a sound. More expanding and contracting, stretching, then white light again.

I played the CD "Alpha, Alert Relaxation" and she saw a white meadow in the rain. There was a beautiful meadow garden with pinks, purples, butterflies and a brilliant white light with yellow in it. Something spiraled from a sun circle, lovely, and moved up her body. She felt a gentle massage as the sound moved up. Some confusion arose, so she is deciding what to do. There is a bigger white light appearing as spirals around her head. She went back to the meadow hearing the wind through the pines. She described these kinds of journeys as "being held in the arms of God."

JC's music journeys led her through her mind and heart, and she discovered places that needed resolution. In one session, there was a nurturance theme, about being loved. She stuttered in early childhood. She was able through music to tap into playfulness and nurturing, feel it and know it has always been there. She felt a spiritual presence within. There were dreams she reported to me in between sessions. One was a vision. "….the vision has stayed with me. It is a bit unnerving in a way. The question keeps repeating, is it a spiritual death to self or am I being forewarned of something more significant? Maybe it is just that I am continually dying and being reborn all the time. I like that the best."

JC had many sessions with amazing journeys. We talked about the imagery and there was always the component of spirituality for her. I played longer pieces for journeying. ("Tortoise", Chinese Feng Shui Music based on the elements of wood, earth, fire, water and metal). Here is an example of one of those sessions. Her intention was about intuition and listening to herself; having no expectations. As the music played, she began to tell me; "I am near a big lake with mountains around it. A lady is dancing beside the lake. There is clear white sand at the bottom and flecks of gold. I reach down into the water and pick up a sand dollar. A rainbow comes into the sand dollar in my hand. Now I am floating face down in the water. Trying to open my eyes takes a lot of courage. I want to roll over and look at the sky. Feeling reluctance to do that. I dive down in the water, and a sand castle is there. Digging in the sand, I find a pot/vase with squatty handles on both sides. When I turn the pot over, there are jewels. I sense something inscribed on it. My name is on it. Like it's for me, it is me. And the Lord says, 'I'm the potter and make vessels, you are a vessel of worth.' A note inside says 'Follow me.' 'I ask where?' 'Don't worry—enjoy the dance. Don't get ahead, follow.' A lotus keeps appearing, floats on the water. A lady on shore is doing a dance. I'm doing it too. Slow, arm movements, a beautiful dance. The golden vase is back in the bottom of the sand. I pick it up, holding the vessel. Christ is with me and dancing in the air. So peaceful."

In this next session with JC, she was feeling frustration, grieving and had a cold. After doing some toning, her body felt more relaxed and expansive. I played a piece in the Key of E and she related these images. "There is a happy angel who asked, 'What would you like to do?' I'll test my wings and fly. I went diving into the ocean to see what's there, flying all over, feeling confident and happiness. Next, God and I are taking a walk in the clouds, just looking at everything. I asked, 'Why do you love me?' And he said, 'Because you're here.' I'm in his lap, watching the sunrise/sunset which never really sets.... past Jupiter, Mars...want to go to the end. He said, 'There are no limits.' Feeling the excitement of seeing things for the first time, like a snowflake, or Christmas as a child, remembering how to do that."

In another session, we were working with the archetypes. This day was about Destroyer/Warrior. I played Boris Mourashkin's "Journey into Subtle Universe." JC reported: "Under the water, bound up and not fearful. Mermaid is untying me. Swimming a little ways and not sure if my head is above water. Feeling a heaviness in the heart area. My head is above water. I see an island and I'm swimming towards it. See green and not feeling the heaviness at my chest. It loosened up. A mermaid is helping me on shore saying, 'This is my island to rule.' I'm exploring it, seeing what's there. Am I alone? Are others there? There is someone there, he's walking away from me. I'm following him and he's saying, 'You are not to be part of me.' Felt sadness not going to have help, loss of comfort. We're sitting, talking—Why? He says, 'This is one thing you have to do on your own.' I asked, 'What do I have to do?' He replied, 'Rule your life.' "

JC's husband died in 2005 and the above session took place about a month later. We spent many music sessions on grieving that first year. Moving into the second year after his death, she was working on renewal. The Theta music I played helped her unwind the lower chakras. (The four brainwave states of the human mind are:1. Beta-normal thinking activity, 2. Alpha-quieter, reflective mind as in meditation, 3. Theta-dream state and creative, imaginative state, 4.Delta-deepest sleep and lowest relaxation of the body. Researchers can measure electrical impulses in the brain and verify that music can stimulate the brain to entrain itself to the rhythm). She said there was a whale there. Whale represents breath, sound and awakening inner depths, (see Ted Andrews, <u>Animal-Speak</u>). Some seagulls appeared (represent communication, proper eating, diet and exercise) giving her the information to take care of herself. Her water image was buoyant, floating, being held, being safe. Feeling a rhythm again. Having a sense of new life from water.

Note: When I do sessions, I don't impose my interpretations of the images that surface from deep within a client's psyche. Sometimes a client will ask my help to do that. I offer suggestions, like when one interprets a dream. I have much information on dream interpretation, animal imagery and body health problems. When strong emotions arise, I refer mainly to the chakras. Otherwise, I let images speak for themselves in the way blocked emotions are released and refreshing new emotions are brought into play. Where my interpretive skill comes into play is intuiting what music/sound to play next in order to forward the client's own journey.

Dad—

Once when in the middle of my training, I was visiting my parents and was telling them about my practice of music as medicine. They wanted to experience it themselves. I was a bit nervous being new to this. My dad was a doctor in general practice. I didn't know how he would take this. Would he think this was silly?

Mom and Dad sat in comfortable chairs in their living room. I asked if either had a particular problem or pain they wanted to work on. Mom had some general issues. Dad told me he did have pain in his lower back. I had them do some slow breathing, then played "Musical Acupuncture" which slows the heart beat and breath to cause a deeper relaxation. I played a didgeridoo piece which targeted the pain in Dad's back. The final piece was piano for regular breathing and coming back to the moment.

I asked how the session went for them. Mom felt very relaxed and revived. Dad's first comment was "How did you know what music to use that would affect the pain in my back?"

I told him how certain sounds can affect certain parts of the body. And he confirmed that for me. He was amazed that his back actually felt some relief. I felt my Dad's validation about what I was doing with this kind of music and how it was helping in a safe and positive way. Later, Dad had shared with me about how he practiced medicine. One of the key things he said was to listen to the patient. When he listened deeply to their problems, he was able to counsel and give suggestions to help the situation, beyond prescribing drugs. His patients were very receptive. He helped them to deal psychologically with problems that he knew can cause physical pains. He only gave medicine to patients when absolutely necessary. He was practicing a mind-body approach to healing back in the 1950s and throughout his career.

N—

N was a monk who wanted to use music to deepen in his meditation. One piece of music I played was "Healing Serious Illness" by Kanucas Littlefish, a Native American medicine man. When N first heard it, the sounds brought up all kinds of violent imagery (killing, executions, bombs, destruction). When I explained to him that this music was bringing up serious trauma, he said he wanted to listen to it until he got past the war imagery. A few months later in one of his last sessions, he listened to this same piece again. His imagery was of Native Americans, eagles and mountains. The song brought up grief for these people, their history. He cried over the lack of respect for our home planet. He felt grief because of the destruction caused on our planet. This music piece brought him into a more compassionate place. He felt he could now bring a little more peace and spaciousness to this life.

D--

I was new at practicing this therapeutic music and talking to everyone about why it works. At a get-together which D attended, he sought me out to ask about the music work I was doing. He told me he had heard about it and wanted to have a session. He said he was having difficulty dealing with his father's death. The following week he came for a session. He went into more detail about the time of his father's death. Being the oldest, he felt guilty that he wasn't there, and thought his father was feeling very lonely. D thought his father was afraid because of being alone when he died. With that information, I chose three pieces of music dealing with grieving. First I played a piece that slows down the heart rate and breath. He told me his thoughts went to the time his father died alone. The second piece was to get more to the heart of the matter. D went to the time he was in a school yard where all the students were mingling and talking outside for a break. Even though there were many people there, many he knew, he felt a strong sense of being lonely. In the third piece he discovered the loneliness he thought were his father's feelings at the time of death, was actually his own feeling of loneliness. When he felt and realized that, he was able to let go of the guilt of not being there for his father.

My husband and I were recently (2019) visiting friends and we were able to meet with D at his office. I told him I was writing a book on the sound work and that he would be in it. He wanted to give me comments about the session and how the music worked for him. First he mentioned how his one and only session is still a vivid and lasting memory. He commented how this shows the power of sound even in a one hour session. (The session took place in 1999.)

He said it opened up spigots of emotions about his Dad's death and yet he felt his Dad was OK. D's statement about the session; "I was able to get to move through my own emotional state. I feel much relaxation as the autonomic nervous system* is calmed. There is a blessing from music that helps with my meditation. Instead of feeling the busyness from a hectic day, flight or fight feelings, or being exhausted from the day (neurologic sympathetic mode#). This kind of music slows one down and 'reboots' the body back to the parasympathetic mode+ on the autonomic side. I settled down, calmed the 'tiger', and felt rid of anxiety in my body. <u>Melodies of the Night</u>, by Carol Colacurcio, brings me back to that kind of relaxation."

*The autonomic nervous system acts largely unconscious and regulates bodily functions such as the heart rate, digestion and respiratory rate.
#The neurologic sympathetic mode directs the body's response to dangerous or stressful situations. The body is on alert increasing the heart rate and sending extra blood to the muscles.
+The parasympathetic mode slows the heart rate and increases the resting potential of intestinal and gland activity.

BD—

When I first began to practice with music as medicine, I offered small group workshops to see if others responded as deeply as my initial group experience. I met BD in one of these groups. I began by having them do breathing and toning exercises as a warm up to have the group relax and get in touch with their senses. They all felt a deeper relaxation right away. After that, I played a longer piece for them to experience a dream like state and also to be aware watching what was happening.

BD noticed after a few experiences with this music, that there was a place inside her that had the space and compassion to go beyond fear. This larger place gave her the confidence to move through whatever came up.

At first, I used sacred music that helped her body relax and let go of old, stuck emotions from her childhood. She was responding very well to hearing drums. They felt calming to her.

The Tibetan singing bowls also were helpful for her. She was feeling vibrations in her body and able to feel a flow inside. She did have memories or images too. She knew she had emotional swings.

This was back when BD was very young. Her emotions ran the gamut: sleep then no sleep, energy then too much, giddy or bursting into tears. I played some cello music from "Eight String Religion," by David Darling. She saw how she was busy covering those strong emotions as a strategy to make herself feel like a good person. She realized that just covering up the crappy stuff wasn't really making her feel better.

BD was also seeing a therapist, and we exchanged session information. BD shared her therapy information with me, and I would mirror some of this back to her in our music session. Her therapist sent me summaries from their sessions. BD felt a lot of support through this kind of exchange. One of the sessions we did was looking at fear with the view that it "is not as big as you think." I played a very ancient piece sung by an Indian woman. BD's response: "I saw a woman along the road with beating drums. She saw the wailing of women through the ages. She felt women's strength within and without, like all women who have ever been and ever will be. She felt feminine energy, and how all women are a part of the continuum. This woman was aware of her isolation, not like isolation is usually but she was there because it is what she wanted to be doing." BD was getting insight into her life. Music vibration played a big role in releasing and improving her health. The singing bowls helped relieve tensions in her abdomen. The bowls also helped drain the sinuses. Her ears felt good when she allowed the vibrations to concentrate there. The tabla (a type of drum originating from India) is another instrument that helped her get in touch with good feelings. She described it as a skeleton being played like a xylophone, woodpecker in a tree or a hollow log like a drum. She felt the tabla vibrate throughout her body.

One of her longer music journeys was with the music called "Soma" by Tom Kenyon. She reported recognizing energy and divine life force. She saw a wise man across a pond. "He is in lotus position. I dive into the pool of water and go down with no problem breathing. The pool has become limitless, no bottom, nothing, just all water. She thought, Dive into the limitless possibilities. I can change negative thoughts. Enjoy and relax. Balance."

Another session we worked with her as the "young girl." I played from the <u>Brainwave Suite</u>—"Emotional Openness" by Pat M. Cook. Here is what BD reported: "The wise woman is speaking to the little girl. What the little girl wants is to just be a little girl—no adult responsibilities. The wise woman said, 'She is safe, protected and I can take care of her. She can just be a little girl. She doesn't have to figure out what to do to please everyone. She doesn't have to be the mediator between her parents. 'Love her for who she is, she is unique'. The wise woman is holding her and she is relaxing." I finished this session improvising on the piano and BD reported a sense of grounding, playfulness and balance. Thinking about not getting so serious.

In another session, we talked about an "open heart." What does that mean? The music by David Darling called "Sweet River" brought her to notice the flowing grasses rippling with the wind. She was feeling the ebb and flow of this motion in her heart. Her realization was an "open heart" is not centered on self. It is more about accepting self before you can open. "I'm learning to break through fears and not become paralyzed by them. I am noticing and feeling the inner change, breaking through fears." From another piece "Key of E," she saw "dancing flags from the top of a mountain, the unending valley and she was going to the sun. In getting closer to the sun, it wasn't burning me. It was illuminating me."

All the above happened over a five year period. BD's depression dissipated. She felt relieved of much of her stress. She was feeling more in touch with her body and mind, able to make changes. She began yoga and Pilates. She felt more energy. All in all, she was a happier person.

As our sessions continued, I used many different sacred pieces so BD learned that different kinds of sounds bring release from fear. Freeing oneself from fear naturally results in feeling more spacious and open-minded. "Rhythm of the Chakras" by Glen Velez and "Harmonic Resonance" by Jim Oliver helped her release depression and grief. A Chinese piece, "Serpent," we used for grounding. When we did toning with the sound "AH" she again felt very spacious.

She learned about repairing fractured pieces of herself to come back to wholeness. Tabla sounds worked on her body with a plucking she felt all over. She had the sense of being realigned.

When she became very fearful, we worked on merging with the heart to help dissipate the fear. The "Heart Sutra" was nurturing to her. "Biofeedback" by Janalea Hoffman worked well with calming the breath and maintaining a regular heartbeat. She rested better after that piece too. I have used "Biofeedback" for grief work as a way to slow the heart and breath rate down to 50 beats. The piece "Soma" (means relating to or affecting the body) was very effective and she reported an "incredible lightness of being; nothingness."

Didjeridoo sounds made her feel light, as if they were "boring little holes so tension escapes." With people who have had serious issues, "Bismillah" (a Sufi piece that means compassion) generally has a very calming effect. I found that when working with clients suffering from serious issues, they need to feel secure, safe and trusting. That sacred piece is supportive because of the consistent pattern and repetitive themes.

In playing music and getting responses, the client gets the information and/or images that they specifically need. I have learned and verified from many music sessions that there are certain kinds of music that give rise to not only emotional release but insightful information about the root causes of one's emotional problems. Whatever comes up is always pertinent. Without my saying anything, my clients learn from their own images about what to do and how to move through those tough times and places.

One thing which I did with clients was to help them find their "safe place." For BD, it was the wind, water, waves and shoreline with a vast sky and sun. She went to a cave with a pool. There she saw a golden Buddha in a garden.

BD was feeling wound especially tight at one session, so I played "Tiger," a Chinese Feng Shui music that is associated with the element of metal. Its music is forceful and energizing, full of productive life energy. Her response was "confusion to clarity…as one exercises choice, we initiate our will, develop individuality, discover our strengths and weakness, build the power that steers us, and have conscious direction of willed activity. Only our stuff is in the way of what already exists."

We worked a lot on releasing old habits. She discovered she needed to practice new habits and set boundaries. She found she had to go through the fear of saying "no" or "I have to go." If she did not say "No," she would become angry, fearful and resentful. Little by little, BD was getting in touch with the "little girl" inside who felt hurt. We worked on having the little girl become one with the adult BD.

"Rivers of One," Traditional Sufi Healing Music is a piece meant especially to stir one's emotions. "Shakuhachi" is an instrument with a sound to help this movement of emotions and regulate one's breath. "Karuna" by Nawang Khechog gave her "a lot of energy, dissonant but nevertheless unified, and BD marveled at how the voices sounded like one voice."

Some of BD's comments showed me the psychological depth to which sound can carry a person. Also, how it helps uncover stuck emotions and deep-seated fears. Here is what came to BD as she listened: "seeing the music and experiencing relaxation and calming," "unraveling deeper," "see anger as not solid," and "how experiences help you become more tolerant."

In our sessions over the next four year period, here are comments she made pertaining to her particular issues:

>   --"I'm looking for connection (inner and outer) with meaning."
>   --"I'm aware of judgments I make about myself. Being aware, I can let them go."
>   --"Being a good girl isn't good enough. Who is telling me I'm not good enough—ME!"
>   --"Key of E" music—I felt soothed and sustained. A lot is going on, but it all goes together."

--"Chronos", from <u>Rejuvenation</u> by Dr. J. Nagler.

BD responded, "caught in sound, my brain slowed down and I was engaged with the instruments. I see that I have to be OK with change."

> --<u>Points of Light</u> by Boris Mourashkin—"Aware of how tense I really am."
> --"Collier" and "Wes" by Carol Colacurcio—"I saw thoughts going slower."

Even though there are discordant parts of music, BD listened to all of it with no resistance or negative judgment about what she heard. "Not attached but watched the sounds go through me. My mind slowed down."

> --"Journey into Unconscious" by Boris Mourashkin—"This is a good description (musically) of how anger feels…..like a freight train. Sound does depict anger well—and blows it off."
> --<u>Didjeridoo</u>--"I get irritation and don't want to get irritated with my friend. The irritation is within me because I allow myself to get hooked into my friend. I'm learning to set boundaries."
> --<u>Phoenix</u>—"I feel flexibility and strength from this. Very relaxed."
> --<u>Eight String Religion</u> by David Darling--#7, "I have a big paintbrush and am painting lots of colors. The water sounds wash stuff away. This music works at the source."
> --<u>The Dreamer</u> by Michael Hoppe (alto flute)—"Evens one out."
> --<u>In the Key of Healing</u> by Stephen Halpern—"Looking at old messages my mind is telling me…that made

me tense. I can look at my own mind and decide a more non-judgmental response."

--"Sometimes the same sound/music can make me feel relaxed and other times it can irritate me. I see it depends on what my mind is doing."

Since our formal sessions ended, I have kept in touch with BD. Our sessions equipped her with many tools to work with mental and emotional issues that may still come up. She has learned that she can check her body and mind responses on any of life's situations. She understands about going to the heart to respond from a deeper, more compassionate level. BD made tremendous progress, she used her "toolbox" of methods to support her progress and it has taken a lot of work. Nevertheless, her healing journey left her in a place of confidence, openness, strength and compassion.

W—

She was born in a war zone and remembered being helplessly afraid much of the time. Her trauma and anger were very severe. After a year of working with sacred sound, she had the realization that this life is "about compassion for myself. I've been through many things, and with all I've been through, I can appreciate where I am now without judgment. Just stay in the moment, listen to the sounds of my body, feeling what I feel, enjoying it all. Trusting more and more what is so. Feeling the chains, letting them float by like the clouds. Just being with it. Nothing else. No why, but, or because—just be with it."

T—

I came to visit T in the hospital as he was getting treated for diverticulitis. After being in the hospital for a couple weeks, he was sent home, but developed a fever and returned to the hospital. He spent a total of about three months in the hospital. He was feeling very stressed out about the recurring fever every time he went home. Also, just being in the hospital can be stressful. If you have ever spent time in a hospital, you know there are always people coming into your room to check on you, machines beeping, talking in the hallways, as well as the scheduled medical check-ups, meals and visitors. These make it hard for a patient to really get a deep rest. I spoke to T about his stress. I chose music that would be very peaceful, flowing, and in a slower rhythm to keep his heart rate and breathing regular. After the session, we talked about a follow-up, and I suggested music pieces that could be played at home to keep him as stress free as possible. While he was still in the hospital at the time, not knowing when he would go home, I recommended he listen to certain CDs. We spoke to his main nurse to make sure the music was playing continuously for at least the next twenty-four hours. The next morning, I came back to see how he was doing after a day and night of prescribed music. The nurses at the station stopped me to let me know how much they liked going into T's room, the atmosphere with the music was so relaxing for them too. The patient across the hall commented how nice those sounds were. Not only did T benefit from the music but the nurses and other patients on his floor were feeling the benefits too!

The Cat—

I had a client that did sound sessions for her stress related issues. These sessions were at her home, so I would take along my traveling case with CDs, notes and at least five Tibetan singing bowls. I have about thirty bowls. This gives the full range of keys to relate to any client. It is important to have the full scale range because each person responds to a certain key. (A short aside here: when I was beginning to practice, I went to pick out bowls, and chose what I thought was a variety of sounds. When I got home, I checked each bowl's key, and found there were just two keys! These keys are the ones I personally relate to!! So I went back to my bowl shop with a pitch pipe to get the ones I was missing and now have the full range of keys/scales to use with clients.)

When I had all the things I needed for a session set up, the Himalayan cat was always first to come into the room. He would check out the bowls, nuzzle them and then jump into one of my larger bowls! Making himself comfy cozy, he would fall asleep. This happened every time I had an appointment with this client.

We found this humorous too since her cat was Himalayan and seemed to feel 'at home' in the Tibetan singing bowl.

It is always interesting for me to observe an animal's response to sound. They cue into it right away and relax a lot quicker than we humans can. Similar experiences played out many times with animals and also with young children too.

A word from my husband on Music as Medicine practice:

Because many sound therapy sessions took place in the comfort of my home, my husband has been able to unobtrusively listen in on some of them. Here is his interpretation of what is happening 'when there are no words.'

"Sacred sound touches the receptive listener deeply. Because Carol has not programmed her clients with any expectations, they are free to relax the conceptual dimension of their mind, that is, the discursive aspect that is often busy asking questions, making analysis or forming judgments. Sound is energy, and musical sound creates an energy wave. Consciousness is able to "ride" that energy wave and allow it to take the mind wherever. Sound therapy in the hands of an experienced, intuitive practitioner works so swiftly because the "places" it takes the mind via images and memories are not haphazard. Because the natural healer within all of us is given the spacious freedom to operate (that is without the constraints of talk therapy) it efficiently brings to the surface whatever is timely to take notice of at this very moment. And because the healer within, our divine source and resource, is naturally skillful, there is no overload. Healing is a process, the journey takes time. Whatever the client chooses to report or comment on from this segment of the journey, Carol will use to select the next sounds that create the next therapeutic energy wave. And like a wave that unfolds on the shore with natural completion, the client will feel whether enough is enough for the moment, or whether more surfing on another sound energy wave needs to be done now. In this therapy, the client always feels relaxed, at ease and in control. And because the client's deep inner resources are being vividly brought to consciousness, the sound therapy session is being supported and moved along by energy coming both from without and within."

Quote from <u>The Proposing Tree</u> by James F. Twyman:

> "There is a place deep within me that has waited to hear a certain sound, a particular tone that has the power to transform my shattered existence. I have searched the whole world for that sound, hoping that one day it would drift past my ear and be caught in the net of my awareness, then sink into my soul where it would resonate with the vibrating strings of my heart."

<u>Responses from people when doing a workshop/presentation</u>

In working with a hospice organization, I met many people through their training programs who worked in hospitals, nursing homes or through organizations providing help to particular groups. These groups helped people cope with abuse, suicide, grieving and death. I was invited to share how sacred sound could be effective with their pain, anger, depression and sleep problems. The following are examples of experiences people shared with me during or after a presentation.

1. A friend and colleague of mine retired from her work at a hospital working with seniors. Over the years, she invited me to do workshops with her groups. There was a luncheon given for her and I was invited to give a presentation. I talked about

her invaluable work with seniors, offering them ways to cope with life and health challenges. I explained how sound is used as therapy. I began with some sacred music that helps with slowing the breath. Then I played the Tibetan singing bowls that have a profound affect to open the heart and generate movement and change. When I finished, an elderly man in the front row raised his hand. He said he was a musician and yet this for him was an utterly new way to listen to music. He shared that his wife of many years had died two years before, and he was having a very hard time moving on without her. He had tried different things to ease his grief/pain but nothing helped until he heard the bowls and relaxed with the therapeutic music. He had tears in his eyes. He said this was the first time he had felt comfort and peace about his wife's death.

2. Celia and I did a presentation for a group of therapists from around the state. She was a colleague of many in the audience. One woman had been a practicing psychologist for many years and Celia said she was highly revered. This woman was sitting in the front row. I thought, "Now Carol, don't get nervous about this professional. Just do your presentation." When I got to the part about dealing with a client's anger issues, I demonstrated how music can be the therapist. I asked everyone to think about being angry and feel it in your mind and body. I played a piece of music that lasted about three minutes. This particular piece can be emotionally jarring. Then I asked the group to let go of the anger, let peace fill their minds, and I played the exact same "jarring" sounds. The response was how relaxing the sound was the second time. Some people didn't think I played the same music both times. The woman in the front row said she had never thought to deliberately feel the anger in her mind (like her clients had in their minds); and then deliberately attend to a different, more relaxed experience of calming her mind on the second listening. She said she never thought to put herself in her

clients' frame of mind. After doing that, she could see how much help the therapeutic use of music could be.

3. Another presentation was to a group of people who were transitioning from prison back into the world. I first did some breath practices to initiate relaxation. Then I played, "Musical Acupuncture" by Janalea Hoffman which helps relieve built-up stress. I had the group sit quietly, eyes closed, taking some deep breaths, and then just breathing normally. I put on a biofeedback piece which works with bringing the heart rate down from eighty to fifty beats/minute. At the end, one young woman said she felt the most relaxed she had ever felt in her life. She said she had no idea that relaxation, let alone peace, could feel this way.

4. I was invited to play some therapeutic music for a women's abuse support group. I had worked with solo clients who had suffered abuse. I knew that sounds like drums or didjeridoo would bring up anger. I chose some music pieces first to help with release of strong emotions. Then I told them to expect that during the next thirty seconds they would hear sounds that might make anger come up. If they needed to leave the room, they could. It was a difficult thirty seconds for them, but they hung in there. There was one woman who did leave; she returned when it was over. She said it did bring up too much anger. I learned that the severity of abuse and the strong anger emotions that come with that have to be handled a little at a time. Otherwise, it is too overwhelming. Abuse victims cannot function in their regular routine with all that anger surfacing. They manage by letting some out and then keeping back what cannot be dealt with at that moment. This was a valuable lesson for me. From then on in my practice when I heard a client respond strongly to drums or low sounds, I knew anger was in play. Learning about the chakras deepened my understanding. Anger points to the first chakra. If a child is abused, for example, there is no sense of being safe in the body. The first chakra is out of whack. They tend to

feel abandoned, untrusting and not safe. The first chakra is meant to be about being safe coming into the world. Another example is about a woman and her daughter going to a drum circle. Her daughter walked out because she couldn't take the drum sounds. Watching this happen in my group sessions, I saw clearly how the strong emotions are held in different parts of the body. That indicates to me a particular kind of sacred music or tone to use to help the negative energy find release from that place.

5. After my training, the first group I led was at a hospital, doing a session designed to relieve stress for heart patients. I had a group equally divided between men and women. I always began my presentation with music to help regulate breathing, and then listen to their comments. Next I played some music that was a little stronger. One of the men responded saying he didn't like that kind of music. He said "The Star Spangled Banner" gave him goose bumps. I explained that it isn't about liking the music or not, but about just noticing what comes up as you listen, such as emotions or memories. He listened like that for the rest of the session, and at the end, told me his experience was very different. He said he noticed a big difference, and my comments helped him become more aware. He said, "I understand now what you meant, this really is a different way of listening and hearing."

6. My husband and I taught meditation once a month to a group at a prison. With permission from our advisor at the prison, I was able to bring a few Tibetan singing bowls. I talked about how the bowls reflect a person's energy. I told them when I did smaller group sessions and played bowls on each person, there were differences in the sounds from the bowl. The prison group wanted to experience the bowls. Each man got a couple minutes with a bowl. First I led a short breath exercise to help each man relax. After each guy's turn, he talked about how it felt. One man did the initial breathing to relax, and I played the bowls near the crown of his head and on his chest. There

was only muffled sound coming from the bowl, and what I heard was dissonant. There was no resonance or overtones. I persisted playing, and then heard an immediate change. The sounds were full and resonant and the harmonics sounded clearly. When I ended playing I asked him what happened. Did he hear the difference in sound. He said at first he actually resisted and closed down his hearing. He was testing out the premise of the bowls reflecting energy that I had talked about earlier. Then he breathed deeply, engaged with the bowls, and that is when the sound began to resonate. Everyone in the group heard the difference, so he demonstrated, tested and proved that the bowls actually do reflect a person's energy.

7. T is a certified alcohol and drug counselor. T was very interested in the work I was doing. She was in charge of a group who needed methods to relax and de-stress. These were people who were just out of prison. They were learning coping methods to find there way in life, to support themselves and renew their participation in society. T was interested in how this sacred sound would work. One of the sessions I did was with a mix of men and women of all ages. Many had dealt with alcohol and drugs as users and providers. I began with the Acupuncture music that takes the heart rate down from 80-50 beats. I also had them do some toning and played some music for meditation. At the end, one young woman said she had tried other techniques to help her relax before but never in her life had she experienced this kind of total relaxation.

8. I was invited to do a retreat for a group of teachers. They all came together in one location to participate in workshops on creating peace in schools and peace for yourself. I lead one of the workshops and my emphasis was on "Peace through Sound." About one hundred teachers attended. Most of them don't know one another since they teach in different locations. My theme was to experience sound changing from dissonance to harmony, a natural resolution. All of us resonate with different sounds/voices and yet deep down in each of us there

is a blending/harmony, like a symphony. Sound is a way to express each person's creativity and as a group have beautiful harmonies together. I began with breathing and toning sounds. One of the main music pieces I had them listen to is called "White Lotus" by Boris Mourashkin. This piece has very strong sounds and dissonant harmonies. When it ended, I asked for comments about what came up such as any images, emotions or memories. Many had very personal and intense responses or they saw a different, more compassionate way to respond to their peers or a student. At the end, a lot of the teachers came up to comment on how powerful this session was. One of the most poignant comments a teacher made was that he had no idea his peers had such intense and personal thoughts and insights. Others mentioned they felt closer to their peers after hearing these responses. There was a greater sense of respect after hearing what others experienced. It felt to me that some walls were knocked down, and a warmth prevailed. The natural resolution was a definite movement towards greater understanding, forgiveness and compassion for others.

9. This organization thought that music would be a good way for communication. The counselors worked with such issues as: 1) What are the differences between adoptive parenting and parenting birth children? 2) How is adoption spoken about at home? 3) How do you handle your adoptive child's culture when it is different from your own? Music is a universal language, so my topic was about "Listening is Key", "How Do We Listen" and "What Do We Hear?" With the diversity of these families, I came from the point of view of an orchestra, in which there are many different instruments with different sounds and many musicians. The orchestra as a group has to listen to each other and watch the cues of the conductor to play at the same tempo, create the appropriate dynamics (loud and soft) and stay together. Each instrument is an important voice in the orchestra.

Music can help us understand why a child reacts a certain way. I asked them to consider questions such as: "What did you hear? How did you feel? Why did you have that reaction?" Music can be used as a tool for conversation. In truly listening to a child, you can hear where he/she is coming from. To do this it is especially important to quiet your own judgments, like putting them in brackets and up on a shelf for the moment. How a child listens and responds is key to what they are learning and how they process life. When one listens correctly, there is better attention span, posture, and both physical and mental movement. Sound excites the brain which is stimulating for children. The result of this stimulation is an organization of the entire central nervous system and body to improve language and movement. In the indigenous tradition of Africa, when the children are born, a song is sung for them about who they are.

10. I was invited to a school that worked with children with special needs. I had a group of six middle school boys and girls and each had a teacher as their guide. They were working on an art project, and put that aside to listen to the music I had prepared. One young girl kept doing her art project. Her teacher encouraged her to participate, but she refused. I told the teacher that it was okay because she would be hearing the music. The other children were excited about these new instruments I brought for them to play, such as a rain stick, Tibetan singing bowls and tingshas. I then played a music piece to help with releasing strong emotions and asked them what they thought about that. Our time ended, and as I was packing up my gear, the teacher who was with the little girl who refused to participate, wanted to show me the art work the girl did. It was a popsicle stick with a round thick paper glued to the top of the stick. One side of the paper had her artwork. The teacher then turned the paper to the other side. There was a list the girl had made that read: 1. I feel angry 2. I let it go 3. I feel much better. She had heard the music and

responded with her comments; that is exactly how a music session works. What amazed and excited her teacher so much was that, up to this point, the girl was only able to express one emotion. This list of three points was a new development for her. She was able to express her strong anger, and then naturally release that energy. Her teacher said she had never come to a conclusion that way before. I was very excited to hear this. I saw what power healing music can have. This confirmed for me again of how sacred, healing music works when there are no words.

This is an example of how I put together ideas for workshops.

1. This workshop's subject was "Listening with the Heart, Healing Sounds." The focus was on the heart. The heart relates to the fourth chakra which is mainly about love but also learning to open and listen. This is not just listening to the heart but listening from the heart. The heart chakra is the "hub" center connecting the body and mind. The heart is the place we can rest as well as grow from, like a plant rooted in the ground and reaching up to the sky. It is the locus of all characteristic qualities. The heart is the garden, if you will, where we nurture what we have learned about love. Knowing one's heart, one understands better how to respond to experiences and challenges.
2. Questions to notice in listening to particular music pieces for the heart. Why does our heart feel blocked or shut down at times? Where is the block coming from? Is it emotional such as sadness, anger, anxiety, fear, guilt, etc. Are thoughts and/or deep-seated beliefs in the way? How to unblock the heart and mind? Try this exercise: Since our energy usually is with our thoughts, thinking about what we need to do, where we are going, planning, etc., direct those thoughts, away from your

heart. Consciously direct them into your hands or feet, and notice what happens.

Bodily movement of the shoulders helps to open the heart. Try rolling the shoulders forward then backwards. Movement of inner breath sends sacred vibration immediately to the heart. The particular Bija mantra for the heart is YAM. The Bija mantras are sacred Sanskrit syllables that are meant to change, open and create space for particular areas of the body. Focus on the heart and the color green, take a breath, then chant YAM until you run out of breath. Take another breath and repeat for a couple minutes. Relax after that and notice how the heart area feels. This exercise can be repeated twice a day for five to ten minutes.

3. Another heart exercise called "talk/listen" is done with a partner. Sit directly looking at the other person. One person gets to talk about whatever they wish for three minutes while the other person just listens. Then change places so that the one talking becomes the listener. As the listener, breathe into your heart and your belly, *just listening* and not thinking about anything. After doing this exercise ask yourself, "is it harder or easier to offer advice or to identify with your friend's feelings? Did you/your friend feel heard? Do you feel more warmth for your friend?" That is a good beginning on listening with the heart.

4. When we want to close down and just don't want to feel, opening the heart is a practice that can help keep it open and flowing. When we want to close down, we just don't want to feel. "I" becomes too much. The power of Empathy is a way to open and listen with the heart. To open to another's pain/suffering—that has us reach far beyond the boundaries of ourselves. Opening up to the suffering of another is also a way to heal ourselves.

Let's experiment with this:

A. Think of something painful.
B. Hold those feelings in your heart.
C. Tap into the divine energy that is always there (love and compassion).
D. Breathe deeply and let yourself feel these emotions.
E. Deeply realize that your heart is big and strong enough to embrace these feelings.
F. Let love and reverence emanate from your heart, surrounding all the suffering.

At this point, my choice of music for this kind of exercise is a meditative kind of music. One example is from Health Journeys, <u>Music for Meditation</u> by Steven Mark Kohn.

To consider more on this topic, here is "Going Deeper into the Heart."

A. The first way to work with opening the heart is by connecting with ourselves. The heart is about integration and peace. It is the strong need for love—all of us want that. It sounds simple but we all have our wounds and scars that affect our hearts. Without love, there is no binding force to hold the world together. There is no integration—there is dis-integration.
B. To expand and deepen the connection with ourselves, we need to be able to love our own self then we will be able to open to others. Entering and listening to the heart is coming into self-reflection, to quiet the mind. It takes careful, distinct inner listening to hear the mind and body's messages. Because of the busyness that takes place constantly, we don't hear it. But as one tunes in, and hears the constant chatter but doesn't engage it, one can release tensions, uncover

memories and complete unresolved emotions. This is what brings integration and connection arising from one's deeper core within. Notice how much easier it is to find meaning in life when one feels deep integration and inter-connection.
C. Self-acceptance, forgiveness and especially compassion are the healers that allow us to reconnect to our core.

Quote by Chogyam Trungpa—"To develop love—universal love—one must accept the whole situation of life as it is—the light and the dark…"

Using Music to Support the Grieving Process

Grief is about change. Sometimes no words are adequate to express the emotional, spiritual, psychological and physical experience that is grief. Because music likewise is an emotional, psychological, spiritual and physical experience, it can help one to express reactions to life changes without judgment or negative commentary. Having the appropriate sounds or music to accompany the changing emotions of grief over time can be a relief, especially to those dealing with the losses that come with aging.

As a sound practitioner, I use music as medicine to help heal anyone going through grieving. The music I use in my practice comes from the sacred tradition of indigenous sound healers. These sounds are powerful, meant to promote change and give the psyche a place to rest in stressful, painful times. The sounds and music pieces are created for specific issues and bring out the emotions that need to be expressed and resolved. This kind of music has deep spiritual roots, directed to people's inner consciousness. The indigenous music healers who create this music are masterful psychologists and physicians who understand which sounds to use to bring about emotional and physical balance.

For the sake of simplicity, I have divided the grief process into three time frames to clarify where people are with their grief, so I can treat them with the appropriate sounds.

Raw Grief. The first stage after a loss is raw grief, which can include feelings of shock, anger, numbness and pain. For elders in this state, I use music or sounds to help stabilize and provide support for the body rhythms such as breath and heartbeat.

Middle Grief. The next stage, middle grief, puts people on an emotional roller coaster. With the reality of a death or other loss setting in, elders need space to feel. Music can reflect the ups and downs of emotions of middle grief because it is filled with changes such as high and low sounds, fast and slow tempos, dissonant and harmonic sounds, strong and easy rhythms, and soft and loud sounds. Using music at this stage can provide some clarity to the grieving process. It gives the person the space to feel the changing emotions without judgment and without getting stuck.

Mature Grief. Mature grief is a time of integration and making meaning. The music I use for in this stage provides spiritual support and helps a person reconnect to the divine within.

What Happens in the Sessions. In an individual music session, the person describes how they feel and where they feel emotionally stuck or in physical pain. I use sound methods to hear where the emotional obstacles are. For example, I will have my client make sound while I listen for the range of highs and lows. Some people are missing low sounds; others cannot make sounds in the higher range. These limits indicate to me where the person has obstacles. Using this information, I choose specific pieces of music, sometimes making use of Tibetan singing bowls or improvising on the piano to give them the needed sounds. Once the person progresses to being able to make certain sounds, feeling the physical vibrations or connecting with them emotionally, a release will take place. Human bodies resonate with certain sounds to stabilize and reestablish harmony and balance.

Such healing music helps one touch the sacred within and reestablish that relationship to bring healing. Music can augment talk therapy by putting the person deeply in touch with grief without their having to struggle for words or edit themselves, thus helping them experience and eventually verbalize difficult emotions.

In my work, I have found that grief has many emotional dimensions. When grief leads to depression, for example, some people experience depression with anger; others experience depression with sadness. The music I choose for treatment differs in each of these cases. The appropriate music reflects where the person is, allowing the feelings to come up, be experienced and finally be released with some resolution.

The experience from the music sessions is unique to each person. Individuals respond to music and sounds with different images, memories, colors and even archetypes. What is important to remember is that these images touch a deep place in the psyche that allows memories, images or feelings to occur. The specific information one may get from this process is exactly what they need to help them put the pieces together, see what's happening and work through the changes associated with loss and grief.

How Music Helps. A woman in raw grief came to do music work with me four months after her husband had died. She expressed overwhelming sadness, so we started with music that let her experience that sadness. While crying, she forcefully said, "Why did you leave me?" She had no idea that she felt angry at her husband about his death.

We then used music to dissipate the anger. I played a Tibetan chant and she heard the chanter saying "Give me the anger, give me the anger." She found that mentally giving the anger over to the chanter was a safe way to express this negative feeling toward her dead husband. If anger came up again, she would recall the chanter asking her to "give me the anger." These sessions gave her the power to be her own guide and effectively work through her thoughts and emotions.

Sacred music is created with the intention of helping people deal with change, so it is especially effective for dealing with the grieving process. Such music is supportive and allows for expansiveness. It can help one find meaning in their experiences because it helps them recognize and integrate difficult emotions. One who has experienced loss can find strength in the imagery evoked from music when they connect that information to what is happening in their lives. In doing so, they are taking responsibility for their own healing.

Grief and Using Specific Music for Release: The Bija Mantras

The grief process is filled with a wide range of emotions. The process often includes feelings of being out of control. When these feelings become overwhelming it can be difficult or scary to get in touch with them. Music is used effectively as a means of accessing feelings that seem stuck or numbed. Music stimulates images and memories providing a non-verbal and often a more powerful means of experiencing a loss. Music by-passes the conceptual mind that is filled with busy chatter and judgements, and gives the psyche a place to rest when times are painful and stressed.

Adjusting to life without a loved one can give rise to many uncomfortable feelings and unpleasant issues. Playing music that supports and matches a person's need to vent or gain insight can normalize their feelings and provide a safe structure for expression. Whether the grieving client is depressed, angry, confused or lonely, music has the power to generate the movement and dynamics to keep their process moving towards some comforting resolution. Using music consciously and with deliberate purpose can help that atmosphere and support needed, providing feelings of power and control rather than avoidance.

Many things may surface when using music during the grieving process. For example, it can encourage the person to feel the feelings, relieve memories and release on a physical level. Old grief may come up, and this can be a vulnerable time but also a powerful time of growth. To allow answers to emerge and to feel connected is important for movement along one's spiritual path.

The music I use for grief work can vary considerably since it depends on the way a person is experiencing grief. Some people are angry, others are depressed and lonely. Some have pain and tension, while for others spiritual issues are raised and they grasp for the answer to the question "Why?"

These are all different states of mind and the music used must be chosen specifically with that emotion or thought process in mind. For example, for anger, tension and pain, I would use stronger sounds, with rhythmic patterns that would slow the breathing, release tension and calm brain waves. Different tones, strong rhythms and medium/fast tempos help relieve physical stress and bring one back to normal breathing patterns. This slowing of the breath and deep breathing can reduce blood pressure to create a calmer state of mind. The music is the "medicine" because it is acting as a non-invasive, non-synthetic chemical sedative.

Examples of music I have used for anger are "Musical Acupuncture" by Janalea Hoffman, "Points of Light" by Boris Mourashkin, "Tibetan Singing Bowls" by Carol Colacurcio, "Rivers of One" by The Rast Makam (Sufi healing Music). For slowing the breath. "Harmonic Resonance" by Jim Oliver, "Soma" by Tom Kenyon, "Piano Concerto #21", 2nd movement (Elvira Madigan) by Mozart and also there are CDs with sounds of nature. For spiritual issues I have used "Conversations with God" #11 by Liz Story, "In Paradisum" by Faure, and "Rosa Mysctica" by Therese Schroeder-Sheker.

The Bija mantras are a vocal way to vibrate specific places in the body. Bija is Sanskrit for "seed" which vibrates with the energy of that particular area (chakra). Mantra ("Man" means to think and "tra" means to liberate) focuses concentration and calms and stills the mind. These are sounds that create transformation. This is done by sound waves that resonate at specific vibration frequencies. Every cell in our body can be rejuvenated using mantra. The sound resonates perfectly because our body is mainly composed of water which is a sound resonator. This creates spaciousness within one's body and mind allowing one to feel safe, protected and courageous, especially in very difficult times.

Celia

I had first begun doing music work in the hospice organization and began by visiting patients. Celia heard about the music work I was doing with patients through our director in hospice. Celia was a grief therapist. She led a cancer group each week and invited me to give a music presentation for the kind of issues her group was dealing with. They responded positively to the session. They commented on how quickly their breathing slowed down which led to deeper relaxation in the body. Most got images from certain time in their lives, or they took a virtual journey back to a particular past event. The particular image a person may get has something to do with a change in emotions or mental shift. When I asked more questions about the imagery, they could identify them as places that set them in a certain direction (maybe a breakup in the family that caused anger or a sad event that clouded their mind with loneliness. Note: a severe stress-related event can sometimes be the trigger for the onset of cancer). Celia was amazed at how quickly this kind of music could affect a person. She commented to me that talk therapy takes a long time to get to the heart of the matter. She saw how music cuts through or bypasses the mental busyness and other conceptual obfuscations and gets to the core dynamic where change can be made.

Later she set up a few appointments with me to really experience this sound work more personally and deeply for herself. One of her main issues was the difficult relationship with her mother. She was angry with her mother most of the time. It was difficult for Celia to communicate with her, and eventually even minimal communication stopped. However, she never felt sad about losing the relationship with her mother, and she never shed a tear. We did a series of sessions and around the fourth one, she did cry. She was so happy that she could finally shed a tear for her "Mum."

A few years later, she visited her mother and Celia noticed her own anger was not there. She could listen to her mother and know the anger was her mother's, not hers. She and her mother were able to be together in peace. Her mother died soon after this reconciliation.

Celia-Workshops

After Celia's sessions, we decided to work together creating workshops. Celia's work covered a range of issues. Besides the grief felt after losing a loved one, she counseled clients who tried to commit suicide or the family who lost someone to suicide. She did work with a special group that did weekend retreats to work through issues around abortion. She invited me to attend to see what came up for these women and how they were working through it. One major important thing I learned from serious issues like these is that it takes a lot longer to unravel the mental/emotional traumas.

Other areas she involved me in were conferences on death and dying as well as bereavement. This was helpful since I was doing music sessions with hospice patients. Through these conferences I was able to see a larger range of responses people have when grieving and after a death. We attended ADEC (Association for Death Education and Counseling) conferences every year. Celia gave a presentation on coping with loss. I gave a presentation on using cross cultural music or toning to help release stress.

At one of the ADEC events, we met with the organizer of the next world bereavement conference. She heard of our work together, and asked us to come to the world conference to do some presentations. In 2005, traveled to Vancouver for the World Bereavement Conference which takes place every four years.

Our presentation outlines had been sent ahead in advance. Celia did a class on coping/memorializing after a death. I did a class on using Tibetan singing bowls for healing. There were over seventy-five people in my class, all circled around me, and it felt overwhelming at first. I relaxed and did the presentation as if it was one on one. A lady raised her hand and asked if I would play the bowls over her. She joined me in the middle and lay down on the floor. Before beginning, I asked if she wanted to tell me anything, but at first she did not. I said that was fine and began to have her do some deep breathing. I placed the bowls at her feet, along the side of her body and at the top of her head. She stopped me then and said she wanted to tell me what was going on. Her son had committed suicide a few years before and she was experiencing immense sorrow and grief. I had her close her eyes and do steady breathing. I played the bowls around her first singly, then all of them ringing together. I also placed bowls on her body to play them. It is even more beneficial to feel the physical vibration of the bowls as well as hear the auditory vibrations. After about fifteen minutes, I stopped. She slowly opened her tear-filled eyes. She said something powerful happened and she felt release as well as relief.

Celia and I together did a presentation called "Sounds of Grieving." Celia did a brief description of William Worden's "Four Tasks of Grief" (reality, feelings, adjusting, reinvesting). She also talked about how grief changes over the years. The issues are very different immediately after a death and as time goes by other feelings are triggered. Adjusting to life without a loved one brings up different issues. I gave a description on music as change which can reflect the changing emotions one experiences in grief. Playing music for loneliness, anger and other emotions supports a person's need to vent. Giving vent helps normalize their feelings and provide a safe structure within which to express them. Music gives the psyche a restful place in stressful, painful times. Using music strategically and consciously helps create the atmosphere and support needed, providing feelings of stability, grounding and nurture rather than avoidance.

Celia pointed out how grief changes. Immediately after a death, the first year is a time of shock, anger, unbalance, depression, loneliness and questioning. Music at this stage can be stabilizing to support breath and heart, which helps for better sleep and relief of pain. The second year she called "Companioning Compassion" meaning it gives them space to let them feel and grieve without judgement. At this time, sacred music can address these changing emotions and tumultuous mental states. Music provides a safe, neutral place that encourages letting go of negative emotions. We don't want to shut the grieving person down, but rather allow them to express themselves. Always respect where the person is. Middle grief allows for expression of difficult emotions, experiences in a safe environment. Music can match and support the need to vent. This helps normalize their feelings. Music has the movement and dynamics to keep from getting stuck. It becomes a support to express thoughts and emotions rather than avoid or suppress them. Middle grief may go on a few years, it all depends on the way the person deals with these feelings and how they integrate them. After some integration happens, Mature Grief continues the integration process and provides a larger space to contain all of one's grief experiences. This is a time of making sense and finding purpose. As the griever helps themselves, they begin to help others by having more empathy and compassion for others. In a wonderful way, music allows one to be in touch with grief, joy and peace all at the same time. It also helps move the process forward of accepting, reconnecting and deepening on one's own spiritual path.

Later we developed workshops together on finding your voice using both talk and written exercises as well as focused listening to music. The main focus was to enhance and develop inner wisdom, tap into one's intuition, and find out what breaks old negative habits that get in the way.

Another workshop was on the archetypes. I thought it would be useful to the healing journey if clients learned more about the characteristics of each archetype. Everyone has all of the archetypes within. These workshops were designed to study which archetypes were predominate while leaving the others in the shadows. I studied with Carol S. Pearson who wrote <u>Awakening the Heroes Within</u> about the twelve archetypes. Innocent, Orphan, Warrior, Caregiver, Seeker,

Destroyer, Creator, Lover, Ruler, Magician, Sage and Jester. The study of the archetypes helps one find deep personal truths, and in so doing, transforms one's perception of the world. She pointed the ways we each display strong and weak archetypes. All archetypes are important for overall development. We looked in depth into each one to find where we were displaying the wisdom side or shadow side. Some of my clients found the archetypes useful in seeing their strong and weak characteristics and learning to understand how to bring them into balance. The archetypes can be closely matched up with the chakras. Both of these methods deal with a part of the body and/or psyche that holds emotions, physical and mental problems. When Celia became aware of this information, she found it useful as another way to approach her clients.

Rediscovering Joy is a workshop Celia and I did using pen and paper exercises, breathing exercises and experiential music listening. We delved into what is Joy? Our group named qualities of joy such as generosity, patience, courage, kindness, clarity, wisdom and compassion. We talked about how suffering can be an integral part of the most profound joy (for example, labor then birth, learning difficult but powerful truths). Real joy is based on real effort, not fantasies about how we think things should be.

1. To discover joy, you have to make yourself face things you fear. This will develop courage. 2. Allow grief to wash over you even if you think you are drowning. 3. Channel rage/anger into compassionate action. Benefiting other also has the effect of benefiting you.

In grieving you may feel overwhelmed but you are still here and joy awaits. You may feel robbed, but there will be new memories to be made. You come to know impermanence and how everything changes. It is a learning process to stay resilient in the midst of overwhelming loss. You can learn to hold your own happiness. Even though true happiness is an infinite reservoir, it doesn't come from outside. You are its source. And truth be told, happiness is actually a learned habit. From there, you bring joy to others as well.

Celia's main area she developed furthers was on "Forgiveness." She wrote in 2011 <u>Forgiveness Frees the Forgiver—A How to Forgive</u>

Guidebook. This book was based on a series of sessions over a six week time period. She covered "How to Forgive," the process of forgiveness. Her four steps are: 1. Name it (reactions, feelings, losses) 2. Claim it (restorative justice, apologizing, self-forgiveness, alienation, reconciliation) 3. Tame It (Changes in perception, change of heart, change of behavior) and 4. Just do it! (why wait, love yourself, where are you now?). She talked about how forgiveness was not easy to achieve but absolutely necessary. Otherwise, one strays stuck in judgmental thoughts, pain and anger. Together we taught a six week course. We both saw how each person's mind state became more pliable and calmer. The people in this workshop reported becoming less self-absorbed. They began to notice how others had problems worse than their own. Their concern was redirected and they were looking for ways to help others with what had helped them. Finding forgiveness helped them find a clearer way.

Celia and I worked together for twenty years. She was an amazing grief therapist. She became one of my dearest friends. After all this work we did, she thought we needed to write a book. I had not thought about doing that but began to entertain the idea. Once we both semi-retired, writing about our experiences was a definite possibility. Unfortunately, Celia contracted lung cancer and died in 2016 at the young age of sixty-nine. To honor her, I am finally getting around to writing the book about our experiences together. She taught me so much about the grief process. She showed how much patience it takes to deal with grief and abuse. Her loving, yet firm approach with clients helped them uncover their pain and live fuller lives with greater understanding and compassion. She loved to travel and we took trips together. She was a loving wife, mother and grandmother. She was very devoted in her spiritual life. I miss her as a colleague and especially as a dear friend. She has been a great influence in my personal and professional life. I miss her terribly but know she will always be part of my life.

Hospice—Death and Dying

After having experienced the death of my best friend a few months out of high school, I was struck by the fact that you never know when you will die. I realized how impermanent things really are and there is nothing we can really hold on to in this world. So the question became for me, what is lasting? What does happen at the time of death and how can you work in preparation for death, instead of just waiting for it to happen? These questions set me on a track to meet with teachers from the Vajrayana tradition of Tibetan Buddhism. The first teachings I heard moved me deeply about the causes of suffering and way to end suffering. Also I made a heartfelt connection with the teaching that compassion is our natural state, and our purpose is to benefit all sentient beings. I learned that all problems affecting the human condition stem from our own minds. This began my understanding of why one suffers and where suffering really comes from. I found that to truly be happy is not something one would find by looking to the world outside oneself but actually comes from within. To get there it takes a lot of mindfulness in uncovering and unmasking our own beliefs that we mistake for reality. Practicing mindfulness is the key to seeing through the illusory quality of our beliefs. What arises in their place, since it has always been there, are the qualities of spaciousness and compassion for self and others.

After high school, I studied/performed music at Indiana University. After graduating from IU, I began teaching private and class piano lessons and also did accompanying for a variety of groups.

After I had been teaching piano lessons for years, I felt there was more power to uncover in music than I had experienced so far and wanted to find out about these other dimensions that I sensed were there. So I began searching for a teacher and a training. I found it a few months later, and in 1997, I went to Seattle to participate in five sessions over a year's time. It was called "The Use of Cross Cultural Music for Therapeutic Application" by Pat M. Cook. Her expertise and training is about using sacred music/sounds for healing purposes which the third world cultures have been doing since time out of mind. The songs or sounds from indigenous cultures are specific for healing particular problems such as body pain, sleep problems, mental issues or internal problems. In between sessions, I read all that I could about sound as medicine. I listened to many cultures' healing songs and took careful notes about how I felt. Very powerful images occurred during this time which were helpful in directing my life. I was very excited about combining music with helping and healing people. This was the added dimension of music I had been searching for.

I had volunteered at a non profit hospice organization, and thought my specialized training might be helpful to those very sick, in pain, or unconscious and near death. I dealt with patients who had brain tumors, cancer of all kinds, Alzheimers and at the time of death. The caregivers themselves also found support from the music. At the time of dying, the body is shutting down and the spirit of the dying person is in the process of release from the body and all attachments. For this time, an appropriate response to support them in these emotional-spiritual-mental changes is to encourage this release and transition. This can be done with the appropriate music, which is soothing, calming, and moving a prompt release of the spirit from the crown chakra. I have played the music "Rosa Mystica" by Therese Schroeder-Sheker, which she composed especially for this unique moment. Ms. Sheker is a harpist, an instrument that is especially effective because of the calming, higher sounds. Lynda Poston-Smith also has devotional/spiritual music which is slower and soothing. Her CDs are "Steal Away Home" and Sigh of the Soul." If I don't have access to a CD player, I always take some Tibetan singing bowls with me. I have facilitated many times with people close to and at the time of death. One of my patients was unconscious and all scrunched up lying on her side. I sat next to the bed by her head and saw that her face was very tense. I began singing some prayers very softly and slowly. I had two singing bowls, and placed one on the pillow above her head. The other bowl, I held and played it near her heart. As I began doing this, she uncoiled her body and rolled slowly to her back. She moved and straightened her arms by her side. The tension in her face totally relaxed. I was there for an hour or so and she stayed in this relaxed position.

Later in the evening at home, one of my hospice colleagues called to tell me this woman had died peacefully very soon after I left. Working as a hospice caretaker using the appropriate music showed me that surrounding a dying person with comfort and calm sounds helps enable them to leave this world with peace and love.

Music becomes the therapist when there are no words.

Tibetan Singing Bowls

"Silence is the place from which all sound, all speech arises. Listening to the silence can be a doorway to the natural state. If you have difficulty connecting with silence, this means you are trying to listen to it not through naked, non-conceptual awareness, but through another active voice that itself is noisy. If you are trying to invite, reject or change the inner noise, you are only trying to listen from within the noise itself."
(from Tenzin Wangyal Rinpoche, <u>Listening within the Silence</u>).

Tibetan singing bowls are a large part of my sound practitioner practice. They serve in many ways to create healing. They originally were used for meditation, healing and ceremonial rituals.

The story is that the bowls were brought into Tibet from India in the 8th century B.C.E. by Padmasambahva. The Tibetan monks continued to hand make the bowls and when the monks create anything, it is with prayerful attention to detail. So, the sound that emanates from the bowls has a sacredness that affects one on a cellular level. The vibrations of the bowls are beneficial not only hearing the sound but feeling them through the skin and bones. People comment on feeling the warmth and buzz for a time afterward too.

The bowls are made of at least seven metals (sometimes up to twelve metals) such as gold, silver, copper, zinc, tin, lead and iron. The metals symbolize the planets in the solar system. This combination creates the multiple harmonic overtones. The bowls have a calming and captivating sound at the same time. There is some scientific basis for their effect. They cause the left brain/right brain synchronization which creates a balancing effect.

The original Tibetan singing bowls are unique because they produce multiple harmonic overtones at the same time. The overtones are a result of using an alloy consisting of multiple metals, each producing its own overtone. New bowls can also produce multiple harmonic overtones if they are high quality bronze, but many are made from a simpler alloy and produce only a principal tone and one harmonic overtone.

The bowls reflect energy. In other words, they will vibrate according to the energy of the person, and this reflected energy can be used as a diagnostic tool. In working with the bowls, I will place them directly on clients or around them in close proximity. One woman who was interested in sound therapy came for a session. When I do a first session for someone, I check breathing, toning and use some of the singing bowls to hear what sounds arise. I was able to place a medium bowl on her abdomen and a smaller bowl below her throat along with a bowl at her feet and one near her crown. The bowls do not need to be in direct contact. I began playing the bowls by gonging them or make them sing by running the mallet around the rim of the bowl. The sounds that come are a reflection of the person's energy. She was sounding very good, a nice combination of range in sound. Then I played the bowl near her throat and there I only heard a clunking sound, no resonance or overtones. Even though I played the bowl for quite some time, I could not get it to ring clear and pure. So, I asked her if she had something going on there. She was not aware of anything. I suggested when she visit her doctor next to let him know about this. About two weeks later, she told me she had seen her doctor who did some tests on that area and found a hernia. She was amazed how just the sound of the bowl was different and indicated a problem. I had her listen to how different the sound was there compared to the other bowls.

There are many ways to listen to what is happening. One can focus on the sound as many faceted or as just one tone. Sometimes several sounds emerge with a particular rhythm (like a wa-wa cry). This happens when people are stressed and anxious. Their body is absorbing the low sounds and vibrations while the high sound is still "singing."

All life is vibration. All dis-ease is discordant vibration. The singing bowl's vibrations and sounds have a very profound effect on the body, mind and spirit. In hearing the bowls, one is surrounded by the sounds and feels more composed and at one. Discordant vibrations can be changed and healed to the cellular level. In a group workshop, I was demonstrating different toning sounds and playing the bowls. When I asked for responses of how they felt, one woman told me she had gotten a headache from the music. I talked about how sound is like water and wants to flow but if the sound gets to a tense place in the body (like water flowing around a rock), it will accentuate the tension. We did some relaxing breathing and I asked her to go along with the rest of the session. At the end of the session, she came up to tell me her headache was gone.

The sound of the bowls resonates in us. They give rise to an alert state yet relaxed, as in meditation or yoga. Because this state goes beyond the logical mind, one is able to relax deeply and release the conceptual busyness and clamor. In this calmer state, memories, images and emotions can arise and be released or integrated. When I work with groups of people, an interesting phenomenon happened every time. Each person in the group would choose a bowl. At the same time, I asked everyone to play their bowl. At first the sounds were very cacophonous and dissonant. Within about three minutes of continuing to play, the sound would even out and become harmonious. Everyone heard it and they were quite pleased. This is a wonderful example of entrainment. The bowls did not remain dissonant but sounded in harmony which was a reflection of the group coming into harmony.

Healing takes place because of this reconnection to one's own essential center that is naturally healthy and whole.

These kinds of sacred sounds can uncover hurt and blocked places in a gentle, supportive way that frees them for either release or integration. For example, in playing the singing bowls, the response to the sounds was feeling free and flowing especially in the head area. It was like water cleansing the mind and washing away negative thoughts and emotions. One is left with a sense of being purified. This can lead the mind to the fundamental qualities of compassion and new perspectives on life.

I will also use many bowls at one time to hear particular sounds together. In the beginning, the harmonies will be somewhat dissonant but as the session continues, the harmonies also change and come together. For example, one client had back pain so I used a few bowls on his back and around him. I kept playing until I heard a change in the sounds. When I stopped, he asked me how I knew the pain had stopped. The bowls reflected his release of the pain, and so I knew at once that his physical state had changed.

Resting the bowls directly on a person adds another dimension, that of physical vibration. Actually feeling the vibration along with hearing the sound, helps people to breathe and begin to recognize where their constrictions might be. One client mentioned that she knew she was feeling tightness. Listening to the bowls and responding to their vibrations, she could recognize that tightness in her throat and became aware of how tight this area was.

It is important, I think, to emphasize how the bowls can be a diagnostic tool. Because they reflect the energy of the person, I can hear what kinds of sounds they need to bring them back into balance. When I have used bowls on clients, not only do they reflect physical pains but also places where one might be stuck emotionally. The sound will be very different with these kinds of problems.

I have also used bowls with the dying and at the time of death. I will place a bowl by the top of the person's head and hold one myself. I then play them softly and have seen an unconscious person unfold from a fetal position to lying on their back relaxed and stretched out.

In playing bowls for people with Alzheimers, I have seen the facial muscles relax.

I have used bowls for people with extreme traumas such as suicide and abuse. The primordial sounds of the bowls are very powerful for bringing one into a deeper connection with the body. People suffering from abuse have so much anger, fear and shame. I find that people each have their own rate of releasing. Some may not want to proceed as quickly as others. In fact, some may not be able to go there at all. It seems that we are like pressure valves that can only let go of so much at a time. We then need to pull ourselves together to be able to function in the world.

"There is the sense of a profound spiritual presence in this rich world of ringing harmonic overtones. The very slow dying away of the sound raises the consciousness of the listener out of the actual sound itself to the limit of what is audible, finally awakening to the inaudible sound within a silence of rare depth that at the same time may be profoundly felt."

(<u>Care and Playing of Tibetan Singing Bowls</u> by Frank Perry, 1997)

Why Choose Certain Music and Instruments?

Music stimulates the physical, emotional, mental and spiritual systems. The nervous system is nourished by sound which is energy. The brain receives and channels energy throughout the body but cannot generate its own. The three main sources for energy are air, food and sensory input (sound and movement). The ear channels about 90% of the nervous systems overall sensory input. Below are the instruments that have the strongest effect on the physical plane, effecting the body through vibration, frequencies and breath. These are sounds for enhancing ones well-being through "good vibrations."

Drums

Drums are a primal instrument and are symbols of the rhythm of life. They create the rhythm which helps the listener be aware of where the beats are in time. Its percussive sounds tend to draw one down into the body. With changes of rhythms it keeps the brain enlivened and relaxed. Drums access ones entire brain and entrain the brainwaves by synchronizing the left and right hemispheres. Entraining is a matching up with a rhythmic beat. For example, when rock music is played, it is hard to not tap your foot in time to the beat. Entrainment has potency beyond just "going with the beat." It is also a potent healing tool for stabilizing our brainwaves, heart and breath. The stimulating sounds that give rise to entrainment are very supportive of the heart which entrains with the rhythms of the drum. The drum is sometimes called the "heartbeat of the Earth". Because it supports the heart, drumming helps release the emotions and reduce tension, anxiety and stress, boost the immune system and helps to control chronic pain. Drums are also very good for grounding. They represent the connection to the Earth element and gravity. The first chakra, which is ones foundation to be born and realize our right to be here, especially responds to drumming. Drumming stimulates and supports the feelings of being centered in the here and now. Feelings of trust and being safe also naturally arise in a drumming environment. When one feels safe and sound physically, the vestibular system (part of the inner ear that provides balance and spatial orientation to coordinate movement with balance) is stimulated, and ones entire body resonates sympathetically. One naturally calms down and the breath slows which helps relieve pain (such as a headache).

A person suffering from abuse, anger, fear, survival issues, suicide and other traumas, has deeper issues and so it becomes more difficult for them to feel calm and safe in their body. There are so many strong emotions to work through before there can be any comfort and ease in being in their body. At this point, drums are not the appropriate sound. They will bring up too much anger, fear and other disturbing emotions which the person is not ready to handle. There are other instruments that can work gently with these issues to help the person go at their own pace.

There was a sound session where I was playing drum music in a group dealing with abuse. I played a piece for less than a minute, and one person walked out because it was too much for her to handle. I learned that a person with this kind of severe trauma, who has so much anger, can only deal with a small amount at a time. I learned they have to wrap it up to be able to function and go on with life. She did come back and finish the rest of the session. For drums to stimulate a safe and calm centeredness in one's body, there needs to be some preparation. Working on one's emotional issues can prepare a person to learn how to deal with later issues that come up. The evidence for this stability is when drumming on a regular basis has a stimulating effect that creates a stable rhythm in the body.

Other instruments that affect the lower body, like the drums, are the didjeridoo and Tibetan singing bowls (see chapter on Tibetan singing bowls). These instruments are helpful because the sounds are felt as vibration through bone conduction.

Music: Kanacus Littlefish, <u>Thunderdance</u> by Scott Fitzgerald, <u>Drummers of Burundi</u>, Native American drums<u>, Rhythm of the Chakras</u> by Glen Velez, Tabla, Didjeridoo, <u>Tibetan Singing Bowls</u> by Carol Colacurcio.

<u>Flute</u>

The flute is considered one of the oldest musical instruments and is regarded as the first wind instrument. Today it is included in the woodwind family. Many woodwind instruments make sound through a reed on the mouth piece. The flute is a reedless wind instrument that produces sound by the flow of breath across the opening. Flute in this section includes alto flute. Flute is played by using controlled breathing and so suggests consistent breathing for the listener. The higher range on flute and medium to lower range on alto flute help to stimulate a listener's breath. Because the flute plays melodies which are a single note following another, the breath easily follows. This gives the listener a note by note line to follow, and at the end, there is a single note resolution. There is a beginning, middle and end. A release can occur, just like a thought that appears in the mind, and one lets it go by without engaging or attaching to it with emotion or judgment. Music that helps one breathe in a more relaxed way helps one to become more receptive. This can be a more gentle approach with a person who needs to unwind slowly.

Some memories or emotions may show up that can lead to deeper issues that cause one to be blocked such as an old pattern of anger. For example: A client of mine had a lot of anxiety and fear which caused him to shut down or be angry with people around him. After we did a few sessions, a memory came up about the fear he felt when he was abandoned as a young child. His mother was not a very nurturing parent. He felt this deeply. However, once this memory was uncovered and he realized the fear and anger connected to it, he saw how that colored his perception throughout life. As he released that emotion, his life became less abrasive and lonely. He began to hear the pain in others voices. Instead of being angry with them, he became more calm, relaxed and understanding.

Music: The Dreamer, The Yearning by Michael Hoppe and Tim Wheater (alto flute), Shakuhachi, (Japanese flute), Karuna by Nawang Khechog, (Native American Flute), Island of Bows by R. Carlos Nakai.

Strings: Guitar, Piano, Violin and Cello

Stringed instruments (violin, cello, bass, guitar) are in the string family of musical instruments. They produce sound by making the strings vibrate when played with a bow or plucked. The strings affect the body. Musical instruments create sounds at their natural vibrational frequencies, which depend upon their size and structure. The natural frequencies of a musical instrument are called the harmonics of the instrument. The parts of an instrument interact and force each other into vibrating at their harmonics, (wave patterns), which is known as resonance. Listening to musical intervals (the space between two tones), can have a healing effect on our body. When we hear an interval, our nervous system and body posture resonate with it. The human body has anatomical proportions that resemble the waveform expression of musical intervals. For example, the distance between your toe to the top of your sacrum, and the sacrum to the top of your head is the ratio of 3:2. This is the same ratio as the interval of the fifth in music. These musical ratios exist throughout your body. (<u>Calendula</u> by John Beaulieu, 1997).

With this relationship between the human body and musical intervals, there is a natural place to work with a person having physical ailments. The pulsations of tones from strings create a "sound" massage which stimulates the body. Just in hearing and feeling the sounds, a release can happen. If a person's mind is very busy, a lower frequency will help bring their awareness back into their body. If a person is tired, fatigued and depressed, the higher sounds help recharge the brain cells, because the mind is stimulated by high sounds.

"Have you ever been annoyed with a high voice? It is because the sound is "narrow" or poor in low and high frequencies. They sound high because they are not high enough. Low pitched voices with little high frequency content sound lifeless, dull and monotonous rather than low. They carry little "charge" for the brain and consume more energy than they give off, exhausting the speaker (for example, someone who is depressed or fast growing adolescents who appear to be constantly tired and lethargic)." From <u>When Listening Comes Alive</u> by Paul Madaule (1994).

The middle frequencies open up the desire to communicate. Of course with many musical pieces there is a combination of all the frequencies. This is similar to the Tibetan singing bowls that have a main tone and many overtones that come from there. (see Tibetan singing bowls chapter). When a bowl is played while resting on a person's body, certain frequencies are absorbed. That is, the full range of frequencies is not sounding or heard. By listening for the missing frequencies one can tell a lot about what the person needs.

Music: <u>Eight String Religion</u> by David Darling, <u>Compassion</u> by Robert Sequoia, <u>Harmonic Resonance</u> by Jim Oliver, <u>The Tao of Cello</u> by David Darling, <u>Magical Child</u> by Michael Jones, <u>Songs to Shiva</u> by Vyaas Houston & Mark Kelso, <u>Soma</u> by Tom Kenyon, <u>Melodies of the Night</u> by Carol Colacurcio.

Tibetan Singing Bowls, Bell and Dorje, Tingshas

Each of these instruments calls every molecule to attention. These sounds can open up deeper levels of consciousness that help identify and change old patterns in the subtle and physical body.

Compared to our western tonality with its major and minor scales, there are more tones (1/4 tones, microtones, etc.) used in the Eastern traditions (India, China, Japan and Korea for example). Their sounds which were meant for spiritual purposes and healing, go back thousands of years. Nevertheless, every person will resonate more or less with all of these kinds of sounds.

The Bell and Dorje are ritual instruments used in Vajrayana tantric practice. These are used to transform our busy minds.

Together they represent the inseparability of wisdom and compassion in the enlightened mindstream. The dorje symbolizes skillful means to transform ordinary experience to move toward our spiritual path. Its extraordinary characteristics are impenetrable, immovable, immutable, indivisible and indestructible. The dorje symbolizes the masculine, yang and compassionate display. The bell symbolizes the emptiness of phenomena. It helps to bring ones mind into more spaciousness which brings greater awareness. It is a sound offering to the Buddhas. The hollow of the bell represents the void from which all phenomena arise, which includes the clapper and the sound of the bell (form). Together they symbolize wisdom and compassion. The sound, like all phenomena, arises, goes forth and then dissolves back into emptiness.

The tingshas are spherical bells. They originated in Tibet and are used in prayer and meditation rituals. When struck together, tingshas produce a high, unique and lasting tone which helps focus the mind. They are used for clearing the mind, energy balancing and space clearing in a home.

To make the Tibetan singing bowls sing, you run the mallet along the rim on the outside of the bowl. When playing many bowls, there is the feeling of surround sound ("sound bath") where the sound is felt both on the inner and outer body. The way the metals are combined to make the bowls is a well kept secret. Only the masters have the specific formula. They are made of at least seven or more metals. Each bowl has a predominant tone. The overtones are set off by the predominant tone. These sounds and vibrations from the bowls help balance the left and right sides of the brain; releasing blockages and stress by resonating with every cell in the body. Ringing the bowls clockwise draws sounds into the body, counterclockwise helps draw out negativity.

There are many benefits of the singing bowls. They reduce stress (correcting asthma) and anxiety significantly which can lower feelings of anger or other strong emotions. They improve circulation and can restore blood pressure. Pain relief (headaches, back pain, etc.) is remedied through their penetrating sounds and causes a deeper relaxation. The bowls also increase mental and emotional clarity. And ultimately promote stillness, happiness and well being.

The Tibetan singing bowls are one of the most powerful healing instruments in their use of sound and vibration. Each bowl sounds unique and the differences come from the size, thickness and openness of the bowl. Some bowls have a strong single tone while others have many overtones. The bowls reflect the energy of a person. In listening to the sounds of a bowl when played on a person, there are distinct sounds which can indicate a clear place or an obstacle or block. When I hear those kinds of sounds, I will keep playing and even add more bowls to help come to some resolution. The sound usually evens out within about ten minutes. The person also indicates a deeper relaxation and so they feel the difference after hearing as well as feeling the vibration of the bowls.

The Chakras

In sound therapy sessions, people report having images, dreams, memories, etc. and I began to see that I needed to know about interpreting and helping translate this information as it related to their particular issue. The chakras are mentioned a lot in alternative therapies. I began to study this subject, and found that music directed to the chakras coupled with sacred sound for a particular place in the body was very effective. (Books: <u>Eastern Body, Western Mind</u> by Anodea Judith, <u>Anatomy of a Spirit</u> by Carolyn Myss and <u>Music Therapy for Non-Musicians</u> by Ted Andrews). So to begin, here is an introduction to the chakras.

The chakras are vibrational energy centers located throughout the body. They serve as "organizing centers" to receive and assimilate life experiences. Bringing awareness to the chakras helps connect the body and mind. They are a way to map out physical, emotional and mental imbalances.

Chakras are doorways into various levels of consciousness, connecting the body with spirit, the inner with the outer. A lifetime of ingrained habits can "knot" the chakras and close off these doorways. Bringing awareness and consciousness to our habits can loosen the knots.

Through sacred sound these "knotted" patterns can be untied. The use of sound is a way to release, befriend, become aware, cause movement and bring one into more clarity and spaciousness. When we learn to produce and direct sacred sound through our chakras, we energize our entire energy system.

Questions: Have you wondered why you have problems with trust? Or how to improve your self-confidence? Does shame affect your life? Do you feel guilty or lonely a lot?

The chakras are a way to identify and work with these issues. They are a way to learn about oneself and why the same patterns keep playing out, how the imprints first left their impressions in the mind.

This process may recapture lost memories, pinpoint emotional/energetic blockages and provide clues to working through them. This process meets each person where they are and goes with the natural flow of your own personal unfolding.

Learning about the chakras and deepening in the personal experience of them puts you in charge of your change, its pace and its growth. When we learn to produce and direct sacred sound through our chakras, balance occurs which energizes our entire system. This produces greater health on all levels and disrupts or "unknots" negative patterns, transmuting them into healthier energies.

Gently and compassionately exploring the areas giving you the most trouble may reveal things you hold onto but need to release/befriend: unprocessed emotions, unresolved transitions or negative ways of looking at yourself or reality. When you confront the original source of emotion, you can begin to see the difference between that and the built up emotions layered on top of the original feeling.

Using sacred sound in combination with forgiveness work is most important to release traumas from the past (lower chakras). This gives one the power to create wellness with a new spaciousness as the foundation. Sacred music and sound has the ability to alter change at the cellular level, which in turn changes the field of vibration, causing balance in the body (for example, hormonal balance and normalizing the heart beat) and ultimately altering one's perception of physical reality.

Why the Chakras?

The Chakras are:

1. A tool that maps out the energy in the body.
2. They help us locate the specific places in the body that hold particular memories, images and habit patterns from early developmental stages to spiritual growth and maturity.
3. They give us information about where emotions are held, that keep us blocked from change and growth.
4. They indicate habit patterns that are not positive and productive. Through awareness, one can change these negative habits. Like working with any habit, the awareness can uncover the root from where the habit developed (early development, other experiences along the way that solidified the habit). An unresolved emotion may itself indicate how to work with breaking these patterns. However, one has to confront the original source of the emotion which almost always originates from deeply held beliefs. Beliefs are not reality. Beliefs are causes for our emotions, not the other way around, as so many people erroneously believe. In fact, this belief (emotions first, then our beliefs) is a deep-seated, erroneous mental habit that must be smoked out.
5. Sound therapy information can help one determine what sound to make, or particular music to play for healing, for release, for stimulating change, for deepening in wisdom of both the mind and soul. Deep healing comes from our deepest resource which is the divine within.
6. When more spaciousness occurs, one has to be grounded in a foundation of truth and/or spiritual path of some kind that will give support, encouragement, and nurture to this new found openness and interconnection.

The First Chakra (Base of the Spine, Earth,)

"Grounding" of the body with safety and trust. This is our sacred temple—a living dynamic statement of who we are. When there is a disconnect, survival in health, money, home and job can become problems. To fully ground, one needs a solid foundation. The main thing to overcome is Fear. Ask yourself;

- Where did it come from?
- How did it serve you?
- Does it make you want to run and hide?
- Does it make you angry and activated?
- Does it make you paralyzed and confused?

Beginning to get a handle on fear, one can come to understand it better, how it grabs us, how we can release and integrate it.

How was our coming into the world—a loving, nurturing mother/father or an abandoning and painful experience? Was there stability or a sense of feeling threatened, defenseless or needs not met? The experiences of nurture and stability develop our sense of trust. When our needs are not met we begin to distrust. From that point we learn to ignore our needs and perceive the world as hostile.

First chakra issues show up in all the other chakras that follow. Without a stabile, solid foundation there is no base for more to build upon.

Examples of first chakra problems:

1. Taking poor care of your body.
2. Forgetting to eat or bathe.
3. Abandoning your own opinion when meeting disagreement and adopting the other's opinion.
4. Not completing projects, dropping out of school, leaving tasks unfinished at work and home.
5. Eating disorders, digestive problems, stagnant energy from a psychosomatic system that is closed vis-à-vis the world rather than open.
6. Fears passed on from our parents because of their background such as war, abuse, loss of a child, poverty issues, and racial persecution.

Strengthening the ground is the most important first step because everything comes from that foundation. This ground contains physical, emotional, mental and spiritual components. This ground needs to be in place to be able to come to a place of fearlessness.

The first chakra is about our *Right to Be Here*.

Physical symptoms that show up in relation to the first chakra are:

*circulation,
*blood pressure,
*rectal problems,
*back pain.

Some practices that touch the first chakra with healing are physical activity, massage and yoga.

First chakra mental issues are about:

*fear and safety,
*survival and support.

The emotions give evidence of:

*anger,
*insecurity,
*self-doubt,
*mistrust,
*possessiveness,
*inability to express emotions,
*inappropriate emotions,
*hyperactivity combined with the inability to make forward progress.

If a client expresses any of these symptoms, the music that works with the issues surrounding this chakra should have an earthy sound. Establishing a foundation to build upon is important to give them support and safety. I generally go in the direction of trying to build upon a person's spiritual path.

The instruments that are primal and bring one into the body are drums, cello, didgeridoo and alto flute. The client can be taught how to use their own voice to chant, toning or mantras. These are all very supportive. The tone for the first chakra is *Om* and the Bija Mantra sound is *Lam*. Chanting one of these sacred sounds for about 10-15 minutes a day will uplift and stimulate the body to affect blood pressure, circulation, breathing and bone conduction. This chakra is the foundation and is strengthened through the sacred sounds.

Some of the pieces I use are Eight String Religion by David Darling (cello), Rhythm of the Chakras by Glen Velez, The Dreamer by Michael Hoppe and Tim Wheater (alto flute).

The Second Chakra (Below the navel, Water)

This chakra is the "Emotional Center" where we learn about relationships, family and friends. This includes learning about emotions and how to express them or how we suppress them. For example, Mom held me when I was quiet, but not when I cried so I learned that I cannot have both love and express my emotions. This chakra is where we store and react from the habits we learned growing up. Unless we make sincere effort to see those hidden beliefs that we simply imbibed as children, we hold ourselves back. We will continue to react the same as we have always done. When we do examine where these feelings come from, we will be able to decide if that is how we wish to continue to act or make a change. When we are able to not just react according to old habitual patterns, then we are beginning to take control and empower ourselves.

Guilt is the main feeling to overcome. Healthy balanced second chakra energies give us the right to feel in more spontaneous ways.

Sexuality is the ultimate expression of many issues associated with the second chakra. Implicit in sexuality is spontaneous movement and sensation, pleasure and desire, emotions and polarity. By polarity, I mean a natural balance to give and take. The third chakra helps the resolution of differences and union of opposites held in the second chakra. It is the "place" where our many and diverse experiences find a harmonious interconnection so that a satisfying resolution of differences and a union of opposites result. Having done that, the third chakra forms the foundation of self confidence and power. For example, one of my clients was abused as a child. She survived by dissociating. She was in a job that was very service-oriented, taking care of others. But she was not taking care of herself. She has since learned to have better eating habits, participate in exercise programs for movement. Through sound/therapy work she has gotten a better grip and understanding of her emotional states. She has learned to love herself which didn't happen in the emotion forming stages early in her life.

A few questions in relation to pleasure, relationships, sexuality are:

1. How was pleasure regarded in your family?
2. Was pleasure frowned upon or indulged in?
3. Was there a predominant message that hard work and self sacrifice were necessary for survival or the means to spiritual fortitude?
4. Were work and play, self-discipline and pleasure brought into balance?

If plagued by guilt for pleasurable behavior or even first taking time to yourself then examine your belief system:

1. What is the belief system that says sex is bad or alone time is selfish?
    a. What is its origin?
    b. Where did you learn it?
    c. Who does that belief serve?
2. What are the effects of the values inherent in that belief?
3. What is your belief and on what is it based?

Physical symptoms that show up related to the second chakra are:

*diarrhea
*bladder and/or bowels

*sexual potency
*constipation and other problems with elimination.

Mental issues take the form of guilt, blame, money, power, control, ethics and honor in relationships. These are some of the issues that show up with this chakra. Emotional issues will feel like frustration, anxiety, fear of letting go, a sense of hopelessness and uselessness, the need for approval.

The music I would recommend with any of the above issues would have a light and flowing quality. Nature sounds with water work well. I did find that one of my clients was afraid of water which, of course, was problematic. Her safe place was the top of mountains, looking at the unending views (spacious). Since then I check with clients about any fears of water.

My favorite choices are "Rivers of One" by The Rast Makam, 'Mars' by Gustav Holst, "Ragas of India", "Karuna" by Nawang Kechog, "Phoenix" (fire) and "Dragon" (wood) by Chinese Feng Shui Music, Bismillah, Sufi chant, Didjeridoo.

The tone for the second chakra is *Om* and the Bija Mantra sound is *Vam*.

The Third Chakra
(Solar Plexis, Fire)

This chakra is about "Ego Strength and Power." After developing our skills at relationships with family and community (second chakra), we now come to the third chakra which is our orientation and self-definition to the outer world. How our ego looks at this point is based on how we developed trust and dealing with emotions in terms of our relationships in our early years. If we had a strong, communicative, loving family we probably have as good an ego as can be developed. If we came from a torn family, drug problems, health problems and abuse, to name a few issues, then our ego is very shaky, not feeling much confidence. The result from that kind of background can lead to low self esteem, feeling victimized or feeling out of control. Here are some questions to contemplate for further deepening:

- What is power?
- Where do we get it and how do we use it?
- Why do we need it?
- How do we avoid the duality of victimization and abuse, aggression and passivity, dominance and submission?
- Where do we find our own empowerment without diminishing that of others?
- How do we reclaim our innate right to act, free from inhibition and shame?

How many of us live our lives dutifully, the way we are "supposed to," always looking outside ourselves for clues?

We are "supposed to" according to what or whom?

Shame is the main block of this chakra. The main "right" to antidote shame is our right to Act.

Problems that occur in the Third Chakra:

-Being too reactive or the opposite of being inactive. Here the suggestion is to think more in terms of being "proactive, confronting the opposition effectively rather than reactive retaliation." (Steven Covey, <u>The Seven Habits of Highly Effective People</u>).

-Our struggle for control and mastery is based on two basic principles: Holding on and Letting go. One of the first places we experience this is in potty training. Self control is grounded in knowing ourselves and responding with spontaneity, confidence and joy. Otherwise we feel controlled by others and we become reactive. If our innate sense of timing is respected and supported, we learn to trust our inner control over bodily expression. The result is self-confidence. If we feel shame from our action, we <u>doubt</u> ourselves.

-Authority:

- Who was the central authority figure during your childhood?
- What means did they use to establish that?
- How did you feel about this person?
- Did you obey out of respect or fear?
- Did you rebel or obey or did it vary at different times in life?
- What form does the inner authority take now?
- Do you cooperate with it willfully or with resistance and resentment?

- Does this inner authority respect your emotions, body and its limitations, as well as the need for expansion and growth?
- How can you bring this authority into better alignment with your life?

If we still see and feel the "big guy" towering over us, we will always feel inadequate. For example, if a child is punished for talking back, then the ego center will find power in less direct ways such as being late, failing in school or acting out with siblings or friends. This is a block to our own effectiveness and responsibility.

Healing work is done on two levels:

1. Internal management of energy within the body.
2. External expression of energy in the outer world.

Physical Symptoms for the third chakra:

- digestion problems
- cramps
- adrenal dysfunction
- liver and spleen
- diabetes
- ulcer
- anorexia or bulimia

Emotional issues will appear as shame, fear and lack of trust. The reactive response from these emotions causes one to be judgmental, over critical and rigid. There is the sense of being deprived and then wanting others to be deprived too.

Mental issues show up as feeling intimidated, low self esteem and lack of confidence. Without the feeling of being empowered, following through on plans or projects becomes challenging and unnaturally difficult.

To keep an even flow, I especially use these CDs; <u>The Dreamer</u> and <u>The Yearning</u> by Michael Hoppe and Tim Wheater, <u>Eight String Religion</u> by David Darling.

The Fourth Chakra (Heart, Unconditional Love, Air)

1. <u>Finding the Balance in Love, Social Identity</u>

The ego develops in the heart chakra as it expands its relationships with others. There is movement toward service to others. The quality is "self-acceptance" which is essential for acceptance of others.

This chakra is about integration and peace. The basic <u>right</u> is to love and be loved. To connect and heal the heart is to reunite the mind and body.

2. <u>Healthy Balance:</u> compassionate, empathetic, peaceful.

Examine these dynamics in relationship and maintaining balance:

    A. mind and body
    B. persona and shadow
    C. male and female
    D. work and play
    E. giving and receiving
    F. socializing and being alone

3. <u>Deficiency & Excess:</u>

- antisocial, withdrawn

- critical, judgmental, intolerant of self or others
- loneliness, depression
- fear of relationships, intimacy
- poor boundaries
- clinging, jealousy

4. <u>To develop intimacy and healthy relationships</u>:

We need to be able to love our own self and then be able to offer it openly to someone else.

<u>Questions</u>:

a. How can we have intimacy with others if we are distant from ourselves?
b. How can we reach out when we are drowning in shame and criticism?
c. How can we treat others with respect when we treat ourselves abusively?

5. <u>To Love</u>: have regard for sacredness of our being, so there is no shame. Shame inhibits reaching out, and inhibits the awakening of the heart chakra.

- acting with respect and responsibility toward ourselves.
- enjoy our own company when alone, honor our limits, speak our truths.
- show qualities of respect, honesty, compassion for ourselves and others.

6. <u>Discover the person inside</u>:

- Witness, having more awareness, which can bring us to the sacred within. This is where true healing occurs.

- It requires conscious attention to change old habit patterns and without this consciousness, we return to our base and then repeat unhealthy patterns. Through self-examination we give birth to the conscious being.
- Entering the heart is to enter into self-reflective consciousness. There we not only define ourselves but we come into relationship with ourselves.
- This takes distinct inner listening of the mind to the body's messages to uncover memories, work through traumas, release tensions, complete unresolved emotions. What is real love and how do we create it? Our heart cells want to beat in unison but we have various internal conflicting personalities that try to take over.

Coordinating our internal relationships takes awareness. We have for example, a nurturing self, a rebellious self, the pleaser, the self that needs success, the self that fears success, a self that needs commitment and that wants freedom from commitment. All these want to "beat in unison" or entrainment. How do we accomplish this unity? They will form a unity when there is self-acceptance and this means all are brought into loving awareness. With this kind of awareness, there is stability and that sets the foundation for creativity, insight and understanding (Chakras 5, 6 and 7).

7. <u>Grief is the demon of the heart.</u> What have I lost touch with in myself as a result of loss/change and how can I nurture and regain that part of myself again? Where grief is the wound, compassion is the healer. Compassion keeps one centered, yet open, and quietly/gently holds the space for change to occur, providing the stability of a container and the freedom of release.

8. <u>Do not abandon yourself.</u> Doing this means a weak 3rd chakra. There is a tendency to get swept away by others, or defined by them or live in fear of losing the self.

One needs to integrate the self to be able to move out toward others. This is what the Heart Chakra is about.

Working in the 4th chakra, we are reaching in two directions:

    a. anchoring and grounding in our bodies
    b. expanding to reach beyond ourselves
    c. perfect balance of these is in the heart.

9. Questions from your early years to help examine this:

In the family:

    a. Do relationships depend on fighting for one's rights?
    b. Do they depend on giving up oneself to avoid punishment or rejection?
    c. Do they involve expression of emotions and affection?
    d. Is communication modeled so one will know how to work it through?
    e. Does one parent dominate or is there a partnership?
    f. Is there consistency or is dad or mom warm & caring some days and abusive on others?

These elements teach children how to behave in the world.

10. These imprints show up later as projections on others. Our response to others comes from these imprints--a template etched in the nervous system over years of family interaction.

These imprints become part of our program, our reactions, beliefs, behaviors and interpretation of events.

So unraveling these primary/family relationships is our hope to find more awareness.

We can learn a lot from our current relationships. (For example, One dealing with emotions of trauma from childhood and seeing how her reactions with her friends today are connected. Once she released these old angers, she could then see how her friends are suffering. She came to understand that they just don't have the tools to help themselves.) Such understanding naturally gives rise to compassion for others. There is the realization that you don't have to respond with anger at what a friend said, but see they are also reacting from their old imprints. Just noticing goes a long way toward stopping reactions. Stopping reactions is already making a change in old habit patterns.

Above all, have <u>Compassion</u> for that allows us to reconnect to our core.

Quote from Chogyam Trungpa: "To develop love -- universal love -- one must accept the whole situation of life as it is -- the light and the dark".

11. We have a "symphony" of internal relationships going on and these can be coordinated and brought into loving awareness. For example, our caregiver, our rebellious self, the pleaser, our needy self, our fearful self, the self that yearns for freedom: compassionate awareness is the key to coordinating all these dimensions into a symphony of harmonious relationships.

Sacred music will change one at the cellular level and can help and support our entire psychosomatic system. With this stability, the ground is set for creativity in the 5th chakra, insight in the 6th chakra and understanding in the 7th chakra.

12. <u>Forgiveness</u>--blame is a barricade. Blame inhibits us from opening but also prevents us from receiving. So we are unable to go in any direction. Without the movement of change, we cannot heal. Forgiveness returns us to conscious responsibility, softens the heart and renews openness.

13. <u>Love is Created</u>, not always felt. Love is a verb. Love is rising above the "self". Without love/compassion there is no binding

force to hold the world together, there is no integration only <u>dis-integration</u>. Love/compassion brings us expansion as well as a deeper connection with ourselves.

If we have done the work in the 3rd chakra, then we have created a place where the 4th chakra can let go and just be.

Healing the heart involves attending to the most vulnerable and sacred aspects within us. When we can do this, we will drop the protective armor that keeps us bound to the ego. Manipulation and criticism will not work. We can only melt that armor with awareness and clarity. Compassion is the state of being in the 4th chakra and it is who we already are.

<u>Physical aspects</u>:

Heart, lungs, asthma, bronchial pneumonia, upper back, shoulder, respiration.

<u>Emotional and Mental aspects</u>:

Feelings of unworthiness, melancholy, guilt, impatience, lack of creativity, suppressing emotions, feeling smothered, feeling a lack of emotional nourishment.

Grief, love, hate, resentment, self-centered, loneliness, forgiveness, compassion.

The element involved is Air and Equilibrium.

Music to work with has the qualities of wind and metal.

Music to Use:

Musical Acupuncture by Janalea Hoffman, Tim Wheater and Michael Hoppe alto flute and keyboards, David Darling cello music, 'Shakuhachi', Chinese music for the element Metal.

The Fifth Chakra (Throat, Sound)

1. <u>Communication, Creative Identity, Vibrating into Expression</u>

Awareness of the world has grown. We wish to contribute to the culture, arts, creative process. What is inside us has had time to develop into "self-expression." Are we creatures of habit? Or do we fully participate in each moment anew?

This is true creativity.

Sound is one of the primordial ingredients of creation. The divine order of the universe, the essence of spirit and sound are intricately connected. On the spiritual plane, sound brings us into resonance, harmony, information and understanding. It is the prime transmitter of consciousness.

2. <u>Healthy Balance</u>: the ability to accurately communicate the truth of one's experience, witness another's truth, and approach life creatively and effectively. For healing: sing, chant, tone, journal writing, inner communication, be silent.

3. <u>Deficiency & Excess</u>

    - fear of speaking, weak voice, introversion
    - difficulty putting feelings into words
    - inability to listen, interruptions, too much talking

4. <u>Balanced Characteristics</u>:

    - a person with good communication skills
    - good at self-expression
    - good in effective listening
    - resonant voice which is pleasant to listen to, with natural rhythms, good tone and volume
    - good sense of timing and grace
    - good free flow of energy and vibrancy (no agitation or jerky motions)
    - very creative life

<u>Physical aspects</u>:

Glands, immune system, hyperactivity, allergies, respiration, sore throat, thyroid.

<u>Emotion and Mental aspects</u>:

Feelings involve fear, worries, doubts, impatience, procrastination, lack of insight, fear of past, lack of responsibility.

One's mental state effects expression to speak (finding your voice), strength of will, personal expression, ability to follow one's dream, and being creative. Not being able to express causes one to be too judgmental, critical, and have difficulty making decisions.

Element involved is Sound and Vibration.
Sense is Hearing.

<u>Music to Use:</u>

With the element of sound and vibration, use music that has a spaciousness and causes expansion.

Examples are Tibetan singing bowls, harp music. Respiration and metal are connected in the Chinese music for Metal/Tiger is best. David Darling's <u>Eight String Religion</u> has a spaciousness and help with the breath. Shakuhachi and flute have qualities of breathing.

The Sixth Chakra (Third Eye, the Brow, Light, Inner Sound)

1. <u>Expansion of Consciousness Vision, Archetypal Identity, Seeing Our Way Through.</u>

We identify with mythic forces, and we are able to embrace a much larger system of being. We can open beyond ordinary awareness which can bring profound insight and vision.

2. <u>Spiritual Awakening.</u> The persona is formed in the 4th chakra--it is an unconscious-social adaptation and we conform.

The 6th chakra is more of a conscious choice of who we want to become. The new identity must have meaning which leads to the 7th chakra.

3. <u>Deficiency & Excess</u>

   - delusions, difficulty visualizing or imagining things differently, "that's just the way I am."
   - if lower chakras have not provided the security needed to let go, we will prefer to stay with the familiar. This results in closing one off from the 7th chakra, as we would rather remain in the familiar rather than expand to the unknown.

- when we feel disconnected, our energy is split off as it is invested in those other images. Difficulty concentrating. Unplug. Need lower chakra balance.

4. <u>Balanced Characteristics</u>

    - perceptive, intuitive
    - imaginative, good dream recall

5. <u>Healing Practices</u>

    - meditation
    - dream work
    - art work (color and drawing)

<u>Physical aspects</u>:

Nervous system, Alzheimers, ear/eye problems, skin, hypertension, neurological disturbances (seizures, brain tumor, hemorrhage, stroke), deafness, blindness.

<u>Emotional and Mental aspects</u>:

Prominent emotions may be anxiety, worry, doubt, fear, feelings of being misunderstood and unloved, isolation and irresponsible.

Mentally this displays as illusion, self-evaluation, intellectual ability, openness to ideas of others, learn from experience and one's emotional intelligence.

Elements involved here are light, luminescence and intuition. Sense is sight.

Music to Use:

Qualities of music for this chakra would involve passion (fire) to decrease the "burning" aspect. Also a jovial and laughing kind of sound. <u>Bio-Energetic Psychotropic Music</u> by Boris Mourashkin, <u>Rivers of One</u> by The Rast Makam or sounds with a water kind of flow, string music as violin, cello.

A combination of high sound of "ee" and "hum" (toning) goes to the vestibular system to relax and regulate the breath. The need for low frequencies will absorb through the skin. I use low sounding singing bowls placed around the lower parts of the body. These sounds are effective for grounding.

The Seventh Chakra (Crown of head, Source to Connection, Divine Wisdom)

1. <u>Universal Identity, Opening to the Mystery of the Divine.</u>

As our consciousness expands, our understanding embraces a larger scope, which identifies with all creation and is inter-connected to all life. When we completely arrive here, there is a fully conscious state of being. This effects all the chakras, so instead of just seeing at the 6th chakra, there is illumination, 5th chakra-inspiration, 4th chakra-compassion, 3rd chakra-transformation, 2nd chakra-connection and 1st chakra-manifestation.

2. <u>Healthy Balance:</u>

The ability to perceive/assimilate information, open-minded, able to question, wisdom, have a broad understanding. For healing: reconnection of physical, emotional and spiritual. Meditation helps break the limited bond with habits/identities and realize the universal identity.

One has to examine belief systems.

3. <u>Deficiency/Excess:</u> rigid belief systems, excess in lower chakras of materialism and greed. Experiencing confusion.

4. The 7th chakra is about merging with divine consciousness and realizing our true nature. Our everyday concerns distract us from remembering who we truly are.

   --we need to disconnect from attachments, illusions.
   --our purpose is to manifest divinity in our bodies and actions. This is the illumination of divinity in all matter, in all of its infinite arrangements. This is where transformation happens in the world.
   --our roots need to be connected deeply to earth, grounded, to be able to arrive at the fully blooming lotus crown.
   --to become one with the divine is to dissolve the boundaries that keep us separate.

These boundaries exist in our mind alone.

5. The prime activity of the 7th chakra is to derive meaning.

In the human psyche, meaning gets assimilated into a set of beliefs. These beliefs become the operating system that runs the other chakras. Interpretation is based on beliefs--forming a continual feedback. For example, as a child, feeling always disappointed. Promises always broken. As an adult, the idea is already formed that no one can be trusted. Beliefs influence the present situations.

Our beliefs shape our reality and then our perception of reality reinforces our beliefs.

6. The outer changes are impossible without the inner awakening.

   --reprogramming work in the 7th chakra requires an examination of our belief systems

--the awakened crown chakra questions any and all of our belief systems.

7. Back to Universal Identity--what does that mean?

Release of the chakras is not to relinquish lower states, but a release of the attachments/habits which separates us from the rest of creation, inner and outer.

Let go of attachments/addictions and trust the universe.
Stop fighting or being in conflict with habits (we think we must get rid of the bad ones, then when we fail, we blame ourselves). Instead of hanging onto being right with blame and feeding your 'demons', become aware of them and make them your allies. Start small, go slow. Be carried into grace and be loving toward yourself.

Physical aspects:

Skeleton, nerves, aches, arthritis, bones, teeth, skin, energetic disorders, mystical depression, chronic exhaustion not linked to a physical disorder, extreme sensitivities to light, sound and other environmental factors.

Emotional and Mental aspects:

May have feelings of being misunderstood, unsympathetic, lack of tenderness, inflexible and insecure.
The mind displays the counterforce of attachment and self-absorption. This causes a problem to be selfless, trust life, have courage, faith, inspiration and develop humanitarianism, devotion, equanimity and spirituality.

The Element involved is thought and consciousness. The basic issue is cognition—to know.
Sense is hearing.

Music to Use:

Music for this area is to stimulate the crown of the head. This creates spaciousness and expansion.

I use <u>Bio Energetic Psychotropic Music</u> by Boris Mourashkin, <u>Brainwave Suite</u> and <u>Theta Meditation System</u> by Dr. Jeffrey Thompson, 'In Paradisum' by Gabriel Faure, Tibetan singing bowls have a timeless and spacious quality, harp music, and Gregorian or Tibetan chants.

Books:

<u>Anatomy of the Spirit</u>, 1996, 2017, Carolyn Myss, PhD.

<u>The Five Wisdom Energies</u>, 2002, Irini Rockwell.

<u>Eastern Body Western Mind</u>, 1996, 2004, Anodea Judith.

Music is helpful in understanding how one can blend and still be an important voice in harmony with self and others.

Summary of the Chakras

1st chakra: (Reclaiming and being in the body). Not feeling grounded. Abandonment. No sense of being in the body.

2nd chakra: (Learning about emotions, how we learn to express them or how they get suppressed). Nurturance of self and others. Mom held me when I was quiet, but not when I cried. So I learned I can't have both love and expression of emotions.

3rd chakra: (Ego strength, coming into your own power). Balanced, responsible, confidence in one's self, can meet challenges. The main demon here is shame and abuse which causes fear. Fear never will let us be confident and playful.

4th chakra: (Heart and qualities). Expressing joy and compassion. We all have a right to love and be loved. When one gets stuck in rejection, abandonment and criticism, working on release of these emotional aspects and forgiveness are key.

5th chakra: (Communication). Speaking your truth, listening and communicating. If one has grown up in an atmosphere of lies, verbal abuse, criticism and secrets, this leads to shutting down one's feelings and having difficulty with talking and trusting. Learning communication skills as well as toning and singing is beneficial to finding one's own voice.

6th chakra: (Conscious choosing of qualities). Vision, perception and intuition. This chakra opens up all the possibilities of imagination and insight. To stimulate this area (third eye), meditation, dreamwork and guided visualizations with music are very beneficial.

7th chakra: (Divine consciousness). To know; awareness, wisdom. These qualities are the effects of spiritual discipline with meditation and much examination into your learned belief systems. Your ultimate guide is the divinity that resides within.

Bija Mantras, Chakras and Toning

(Sacred Sanskrit Symbols)

1.	Base of spine (Earth)	Lam	Red	Safety	Om
2.	Below Navel (Water)	Vam	Orange	Relationship	Om
3.	Solar plexus (Fire)	Ram	Yellow	Personal Power	Ah
4.	Heart (Space)	Yam	Green	Heart	Ah Oo
5.	Throat (Air)	Ham	Turquoise	Communication	Eh
6.	Forehead (Water)	Aum	Indigo	Intuition	Ee
7.	Crown (Space)	Om	Violet	Spirit	Silent

Chakra Chart

Color/Note	Chakra (Location/Function/Behavior)	Color's Effect	Problems Treated
Red / C	1st--base of spine Body, creative, Sexual, restorative Process Transmutation	Energizes, heats, vitalizes, promotes circulation: stimulates adrenalin, red blood cell Production, menstrual Flow and sexual power Strengthens courage.	Anemia, infertility colds/chills, menstruation
Orange / D	2nd--below navel Emotional center Purification	warms and cheers, frees bodily and emotional tension Aids mentality	lung ailments, epilepsy, mental prob., rheumatism and Kidney prob.

Yellow / E	3rd--solar plexus Thinking (mental) Center, ambition Ego strength	inspires and awakens mind strengthens the nerves, helps Reasoning, aids Self-control, aids Elimination, Improves skin, Cerebral and Nerve stimulant	stomach prob indigestion, gas, constipation, liver problems, eczema and nervous exhaustion
Green / F	4th—heart Sensitivity, feelings Compassion/ harmony	Harmonizes and balances, soothes and restores, stimulates the heart, Soothes the nerves, Brain, heart, eyes; Refreshes.	Headaches, Heart prob., ulcers, eye problems, nervous prob.
Blue / G	5th--throat area Communication Self-expression Listening	antiseptic, cooling, sedative, relaxing, soothing, helps stop bleeding, helps with Nutrition and Building the skin And body, promotes truth, Loyalty, reliability	inflammation throat prob. fevers, burns infections, spasms, pain headaches and diarrhea

Indigo / A	6th—pineal Pituitary area Third eye, perception Realization	electric, cooling, astringent, anesthetic effect, builds white blood Cells, increases Activity of spleen, Depresses heart And nervous system	Pneumonia, mental prob., convulsions, and eye, ear, nose problems
Violet / B	7th—crown Top of head Universal consciousness, Oneness	stimulates spiritual nature and intuition, elevates inspiration, expands ration, expands Standing	Mental disorders, neuroses neuralgia concussions cramps Tumors, Scalp prob.

Resource List of Music

Music for Waking

Vivaldi—The Four Seasons
Grief—"Morning" from Peer Gynt Suite
Mozart—Violin or Piano Concertos
Beethoven—Sixth Symphony "Pastoral"
C. Colacurcio—Sound Accord CD

Music for Calming Anger

Bach—Two Concertos for Two Pianos
Handel—The Harp Concerto
Barber—Adagio for Strings
J. Hoffman—Musical Acupuncture
Scott Fitzgerald—Thunderdance CD
C. Colacurcio–Sound Accord, Melodies of the Night CDs

Music to Air Anger

Beethoven—Egmont Overture
Beethoven—Symphony #7
Brahms—Piano Concerto #1
Saint-Saens—G minor Piano Concerto No. 3rd Movement
Boris Mourashkin—Points of Light CD

Music to Help Fall Asleep

Bach—Air on a G String
Debussy—Clair de Lune
Pachelbel—Canon in D
C. Colacurcio—Melodies of the Night
J. Hoffman—Musical Acupuncture
M. Hoppe, T. Wheater—The Dreamer, The Yearning

Music to Relieve Depression

Beethoven—Piano Concerto #5
Mozart—Hoffner Symphony #35
Rachmoninoff—Piano Concerto #2
Nawang Kechog—Tibetan Meditation Music, Karuna

Music to Relax and Relieve Stress

Beethoven—Symphony #6
Mozart—Concerto for Flute and Harp
Ralph Vaughan Williams—The Lark Ascending, Greensleeves
C. Colacurcio—Sound Accord, Melodies of the Night

Music for Energy and Focus

Bach—The Brandenburg Concertos
Beethoven—Symphonies #1, 2, 8, 9
Beethoven—Sonata #3 Op. 69 for cello and piano
Smetana—The Moldau

Music for Meditation/Prayer

Bach—Sheep May Safely Graze
Holst—The Planets
Dvorak—Cello Concerto, Symphony #9 "New World"

Mahler—Symphony #4.
Massenet—Meditation from Thais
R. Carlos Nakai—Island of Bows CD
C. Colacurcio—Tibetan Singing Bowls

Music for Clear Thinking/Studying

Bach—Brandenburg Concertos
Brahms—Violin Concerto
Mozart—Piano Concertos No. 20, 23, 25
Michael Jones—Musical Child CD

Music for Empowerment, Motivation and Assertiveness

Beethoven—Piano Concerto #5
Beethoven—Piano Sonata No. 14 in C# minor (3rd mvt.)
Mozart—Eine Kline Nachtmusic
Wagner—Ride of the Valkyries
C. Colacurcio—Tibetan Singing Bowls

Music for Hospice

Wisdom of the Word Series—Graceful Passages
Therese Schroeder-Sheker—Rosa Mystica
Lynda Poston-Smith—Steal Away Home, Sigh of the Soul CDs
C. Colacurcio—Tibetan Singing Bowls

The above musical references most easily found are classical pieces. This list is meant to supplement the many cross-cultural references mentioned throughout the book.

Afterword

The information a client gets comes from the heart of their beliefs and experiences. Sacred music releases those ideas from old beliefs. Clients share their images and can begin to let go of these habits. This releasing helps them to move on, to connect to themselves with a deeper sense and begin to discover the bigger picture of interconnectedness with all beings. This is a way to overcome the illusion of separateness from all beings.

The instruments and music played are determined by the client's issues. When I listen to what they say, I hear where they are and where they would like to be. The reports of client's examples in this book are spontaneous responses from their quiet mind. Many clients have said, "I don't know where that came from." I then remind them of the initial issues. Next we examine their journey, putting the pieces together, clarifying images, and finding a greater understanding of life's meaning. This leads to lightness, joy and the ability to move forward. These journeys from their minds lead to insights and dissolutions of old habits and beliefs. They are able to come to resolution and find the mind has an abundance of open space.

"It is a kind of music in which time is dissolved in a manner beyond words. This music (sacred ancient music) is able to transcend time."

"Listening begins with being silent. With tranquility. If you want to experience sound, you first have to have learned to experience silence."

"Our 'ears' must transcend their limits, because the 'music' we have been talking about is also transcendent."

"He that hath ears to hear, let him hear" (Matthew 11:15).

These last quotes are from <u>The World is Sound, Nada Brahma</u> by Joachim-Ernst Berendt, 1983

Final Dedication

May all sentient beings be free of suffering.
May their minds be filled with the nectar of virtue.
In this way may all causes of suffering be extinguished,
And only the light of compassion shine throughout all realms.